LAND'S EDGE

A Natural History and Field Guide
to Barrier Beaches
from Maine to North Carolina

LAND'S EDGE

*A Natural History and Field Guide
to Barrier Beaches
from Maine to North Carolina*

Michael L. Hoel

distributed by

**Old Chester Road
Chester, Connecticut 06412**

**THE LITTLE BOOK PUBLISHING
COMPANY
Newbury, Massachusetts**

The Little Book Publishing Company
69 Boston Road, Newbury, Massachusetts, 01950

Library of Congress Cataloging in Publication Data

Hoel, Michael L.
    Land's Edge, A Natural History of Barrier Beaches from
    Maine to North Carolina

Bibliography: pp. 133-137
Includes index.
1. Barrier beach dynamics—Geology of barrier beaches.
2. Predator, prey relationships—Field guide to plants, animals.

ISBN 0-9616080-0-5

This book is dedicated to Brendan

Table of Contents

A Short History of Barrier Beaches 1
    Pirates 4
    Shipwrecks and the Life Saving Service . . .5

**From Agawam to Ocracoke: The Indians of
    Barrier Islands** 9

The Lay of the Land 15
    The Glaciated Coast 16
    The Non-Glaciated Coast 20

The Dynamic Equilibrium 22
    How Barrier Beaches are Formed 27
    Water-Borne Sand .28
    Wind-Borne Sand .31
    An Examination of Sand 33
    Primary Dune Formation 34
    Storms 35
    How Storms Help Create Interior
    Dunes 36
    Barrier Beach Migration 40

Plants of the Dunes 46
    Surface Micro-Climate 47
    Deserts and Dunes 48
    The Genius of Beach Grass 50

**Other Plants That Bind the Sand and
    Build the Soil** 56

From Dunes to Forests 65
    Swales 66

The Shrub/Thicket Community 71

Maritime Forests 77

The Salt Marsh 84
　　How a Salt Marsh is Formed 85
　　The Ecology of the Salt Marsh.........85
　　The Genius of Salt Marsh Grasses......86
　　The Food Chain of the Salt Marsh 87
　　Salt Marsh Pools 93

Predator and Prey Animals of the
**　Barrier Beach** 100
　　Animals of the Food Chain............100
　　Major Prey Animals of the
　　Barrier Beach 100
　　Predatory Animals of Barrier Beaches ..115
　　Other Interesting Predators 119
　　Scavengers 125

Coda 130

Bibliography 133

Index................................138

Picture Credits 141

Acknowledgements

Kathleen MacDonald, Edith Heyck and
Michael Prendergast contributed their time,
and considerable talents, to produce the
drawings, schematics and maps for this book.
I wish to thank them for their patience and
perserverance, and for their excellent advice
during the production of the book.

John "Wild Man" Gavin contributed many of
the best wildlife photographs in the book. We
have tramped over many miles of Plum Island
and swapped many tales concerning the trials
and tribulations of wildlife photography.

The cover of this book owes much to Bill Lane
(front cover photo) and Ralph Scott (back
cover drawing), both fine artists of their
own media.

Susan Schutz did an excellent job of editing
the many different versions of this book. She
went out of her way to be available when I
needed last minute editing changes.

Girvan Graphics, Hyde Park, Massachusetts,
provided typesetting and graphic support
throughout the production of the book.

Most importantly, I wish to thank my wife
Susan for giving me the time and the support
to see the project through.

A Short History of Barrier Beaches

From southern Maine to North Carolina a thin line of barrier beaches lies gently along the Atlantic coast. On a map of the north Atlantic coastline, they appear as a scraggly, broken outline of seemingly forgotten land—where the edge of a great continent plays out in starts and fits to meet the great blue ocean. In all some 650 miles long, with a total land area of about 350,000 acres, this wild edge is part wilderness, part housing development. The Indians used these areas as camping and fishing basecamps, often migrating to them in the spring to spend a summer drying fish and digging clams. But few Indians lived on them year-round for the climate was too severe—during winter they retreated to the relative security of the inland forests. They knew that barrier islands bore the brunt of hurricanes that raged up the coast in the fall.

The first European inhabitants of barrier beaches were generally malcontents—escaped slaves, theives, pirates and other unsavory characters that nobody wanted around and who were content to live outside the law. The law didn't show up much when they had to row a skiff a mile offshore across treacherous currents in gale force winds just to arrive in the general vicinity of the trouble.

The first colonists were confronted with the immense green wall of forest that covered much of the Middle Atlantic and New England coasts. Not much cleared land was available for keeping stock, so they looked to the relatively open lands of the barrier beaches. This turned out to be a mixed blessing. While it afforded them a place to keep their stock, the domestic animals soon trampled and ate the place down to the bare sand. It didn't take long for many of the early towns to pass ordinances against allowing stock to roam free on barrier beaches—for they knew if they didn't restrict their use they wouldn't have a beach left.

This turned out to be the first in a long line of abuses that barrier beaches would suffer. The first inhabitants shunned society and were satisfied with isolated cabins nestled among the back dunes. A little later, small fishing villages grew up in the many coves and backwaters. But these first tentative settlements were chiefly concerned with fishing and didn't greatly impact the total ecology of the dunes or the marshes. Expanding population and affluence brought the first vacationers to the seashore, and they wanted nice cottages with an ocean view—more often than not built right up to the beach at the expense of the dunes. Roads and then hotels and then more houses and more roads; and thus began the endless chain of development that plagues barrier beaches to this day. For some sad cases the cancer of development has taken over entirely. The worst example is the coast of New Jersey, where shacks and vacation homes stand practically shoulder to shoulder along 127 miles of its shoreline. Large sections of Massachusetts barrier beaches, like Plum Island and Cape Cod, the entire coast of New Jersey, sections of Long Island, the Delmarva Peninsula and the Outer Banks off North Carolina have been developed to the point where they've turned into house lots with a bit of sand between them.

But it's not all crowded beaches and hastily constructed vacation cottages built on bulldozed dunes. From the coast of Massachusetts to the Outer Banks of North Carolina the coast is ringed with fifty federally protected tracts of land that are carefully and intelligently maintained. Although the northern third of Plum Island, Massachusetts, is heavily developed, the remainder comprises six miles of some of the most beautiful and pristine beach and dune formations to be found along the entire coast. Cape Cod's National Seashore stretches thirty wind-blown miles from Provincetown to Chatham. I have retraced Thoreau's tramp along the Outer Beach and I can attest to the wild and lonely quality of this beach in winter. Fire Island is a 32-mile long barrier island in near-pristine conditions only 20 miles from New York City. Barnegat and Brigantine National Wildlife Refuges are two jewels along the tarnished coast of New Jersey. Below Cape May, the Maryland/Virginia coast makes up for New Jersey's atrocities by preserving Assateague Island National Seashore, which has 37 miles of forests, meadows and dunes. The southern end of Assateague Island is set aside as the Chincoteague National Wildlife Refuge, one of the principal stopping places for migratory birds along the Atlantic flyway. But the largest single complex of barrier beaches on the coast is found on the Cape Hatteras National Seashore, which protects most of North Carolina's Outer Banks. These barrier beaches are unlike any others on earth, for they arch boldly out into the Atlantic and at their most eastern point are 30 miles from the mainland. From Virginia Beach, Virginia, to Cape Lookout, North Carolina, this fragile thread of sand protects 175 miles of coastline and forms two large sounds, Albermarle and Pamlico. Here you can still tramp for days on the sand and crushed shell beaches, your only companions the gulls that fly in wide wheels against a turquoise sky.

Life on barrier beaches has always been tenuous at best. Bridges and causeways are washed out in hurricanes, and ferry service is at the mercy of the day's weather. Because of their isolation they have traditionally been the home for the lonely and the dispossesed. The charm of some villages on barrier beaches derives from the fact that their original settlers were poor and cottages were built according to the skill and resourcefulness of the builder. Some shacks were built by ''wreckers,'' people who scavenged the flotsam of shoal-wrecked schooners whose goods were strewn along the beach after a storm. A wrecker's cottage represented a potpourri of architectural design—whatever could be found along the beach to nail onto, or fit into, his cottage. Goods from all over the world literally floated to him and all he had to do was patrol the beach and pick them up. A whalebone fence could enclose a porch made from scavenged lobster pots, while the cottage walls may have been built from fine Indian teak. Inside the wrecker's cottage, perhaps you would find an expensive Oriental rug laying on unfinished pine floors. His rude table may be set with fine English porcelain and his wild and unkempt children dressed in tatters of pure Japanese silk. The wreck of a schooner carrying Jamaican rum would send every able-bodied man down to the beach, and the whole village would go on a week-long holiday.

Pirates

Barrier beaches were enticing hideouts for pirates because they were isolated from the mainland, but still accessible by boat. Black Beard, whose real name was Edward Teach, was probably the most famous pirate to ply the Atlantic coast during the heyday of piracy in the 18th century. He reputedly domiciled one of his fourteen wives on Assateague Island. Black Beard plundered ships up and down the coastline, often burying treasure in the back dunes of some of the uninhabited barrier islands off the Virginia coast.

Pirates found Fire Island an ideal site for their own kind of clandestine activities. Captain Kidd was known to frequent the island, and two pots of his gold treasure were dug up from the beach in 1790. Piracy was so common that collusion between the pirates and local magistrates became an accepted policy. The pirate Josiah Raynor was arrested, his treasure seized, and put into a New York jail. He managed to bribe Governor Fletcher with fifty pounds to obtain his release, and his treasure was returned by the sheriff who arrested him!

Sometimes even the isolation of a barrier beach wasn't enough to insure the security of the pirate's treasure. In the winter of 1797 a man and his young nephew went raccoon hunting on Fire Island. A light snow the night before made it easy to follow the tracks of their prey. They camped that night in a thicket, and were awakened by a party of armed men with lanterns moving about on the beach. Not daring to approach the men at night, they waited until the next morning and followed the pirates' tracks to where a cutlass was stuck in the sand. Removing the cutlass, they dug into the sand until they found a heavy cask. No one ever found out what was in the cask, but the raccoon hunter had several large, unexplained receipts in his accounts books the next year.

Shipwrecks and the Life Saving Service

Shipwrecks were a fact of life on barrier beaches, and some areas, such as the Outer Banks and Cape Cod, were veritable grave yards for hundreds of ships. Each shipwreck was a test of man's spirit against the forces of nature, and each became another chapter in the history of that barrier beach. One of the most famous of the shipwrecks along the New England coast was that of the *Pocahontas,* which occurred during a ferocious storm on Christmas Eve, 1839, off of Plum Island, Massachusetts. All on board perished. A local account tells of the horror of the disaster:

> . . . On the 24th there was a recurrence of the storm, and during the night a brig of some 300 tons, the *Pocahontas,* was discovered in the morning, but in such a situation that nothing could be done for the relief of the wretched men who still clung to the wreck. Those on board in whom life remained could see the excited but impotent spectators on the shore, while the latter gazed with useless sympathy upon the strugglers, in this conflict of the elements. The surf was such that no boat could live in it, and those in the brig were too distant to throw lines from shore. The bodies of several of the crew were found . . . . on the beach some distance from the brig . . .

> . . . One man was seen before nine in the morning on the bowsprit, retained his critical position until twelve when a heavy sea washed him and his support away, and he was lost in full sight of the specta-

tors. To make the case more sad, it was but a few
minutes after this catastrophe when the brig was
washed upon the beach, and it was readily boarded
from the shore. . .

Attending to shipwrecked sailors was a mean
business, and the local orphanage was full of
children left by drowned sailors. It was the
duty of the lighthouse keepers to maintain
provisions for shipwrecked sailors, but they
could never hope to patrol the lonely miles of
beach away from the lighthouse. The best sur-
veillance that could be mustered were a few
crude huts stocked with blankets and food, and
sometimes manned by volunteers during
storms. The Life Saving Service, initiated in
1871, was an extension of this volunteer service. The Service built permanent life saving
stations along the coast which were stocked
with emergency provisions, and instigated
twenty-four hour patrols of the most dangerous
sections of the beach. The main life-saving stations had surf boats, life lines, special rigging
for rescuing survivors from the wrecks, and
even cannons that shot lines several hundred
yards to the foundering ships. The life-saving
station crews practiced their drills constantly,
and competition was fierce between crews of
different stations.

Figure 1 Barrier beaches still claim many victims; this
modern sailing vessel lies half-buried in the
beach at Assateague.

Figure 2 Life-saving stations, like this one on Plum Island, Massachusetts, were the predecessor of the modern United States Coast Guard.

The beach patrols were lonely, monotonous duty. Patrolmen walked simultaneously from stations at both ends of the beach, met at a designated spot, exchanged tokens to prove they had been present on the patrol, and walked back to their station. The life-saving patrolmen went out in the cruelest weather, and some were lost to frostbite or were washed away in the surf. While not well-known, the Life Saving Service enlisted men of the greatest bravery, and the Service was responsible for saving many hundreds of lives.

In its heyday, the Life Saving Service had more than two hundred stations up and down the Atlantic and Pacific coasts and along the most treacherous parts of the Great Lakes. In 1915, the Treasury Department combined the Revenue Cutter Service and the Life Saving Service into the U.S. Coast Guard. The Coast Guard has taken over many of the functions of its predecessor, the Life Saving Service. Several of the original life-saving stations still exist, and are preserved in national park areas such as Cape Lookout and Cape Hatteras National Seashores.

Besides pirates, shipwrecks and daring rescues, barrier beaches have been the host for other, more mundane activities. During the revolutionary war, when the British blockaded Boston, salt marsh hay was smuggled into the city to sustain the starving stock. Several schemes to extract salt from sea water were played out on barrier beaches from Plum Island to the Outer Banks. Sea water was flooded into ditches, the water evaporated, and the resulting salt crystals were mined. This laborious method never produced enough salt to make these enterprises successful.

Dredging operations were common on barrier beaches, digging out many thousands of tons of sand for use in making cement. There was never any worry about digging too much sand, because every night the ocean would replace the sand dug out from the day before. The work was backbreaking. A barge would land at high tide, and the men would roll wheelbarrows down narrow ramps to the beach, fill them with sand, and toil them back up the ramp and empty them into the barge. The next high tide would float them free. The men worked from tide to tide for miserable wages.

Pirates, eccentrics, and reclusives have always found a home on barrier beaches. Although now considered a rare breed, occasionally a hermit is still found living by his wits on the back side of some windswept beach. I hope there will always be a lonely stretch of beach on some barrier island where, even if it's only imagined while on a tramp through the dunes, one can live a life of fierce independence.

From Agawam to Ocracoke: The Indians of Barrier Islands

Low-lying coastal areas and barrier beaches have always seen extensive use by man. Before European settlement, the Algonquin-speaking Indians of coastal New England used such areas as summer encampments. Life here was relatively easy; shellfish were plentiful and easy to dig, and the coastal rivers could be fished for salmon, shad, pike, trout and any number of other edibles. The Blue Crab was considered a delicacy by the coastal Indians long before the Watermen of the Chesapeake brought it to market. Game such as deer, moose, bear and turkey were abundant in the forests, and productive gardens of corn, squash and beans could be grown on the drumlins. An occasional stranded whale brought the whole tribe down to the beach for a feast.

The ocean tempered the seasons, and many Indian tribes migrated downriver to coastal areas to spend the summer. Along the coast they planted their gardens, caught large numbers of fish, which they dried and packed in baskets for the long winter, lived in skin or bark huts, and engaged in extensive trade for flints and wampum.

Typical of the Indians who lived or hunted on barrier beaches, the Agawam Indians lived along the Ipswich River in northern Massachusetts. They spent their summers on the barrier beaches that lie offshore the Cape Ann area, later to be known as Crane's Beach and Plum Island. Here they lived peaceful lives, planting their gardens on the high drumlins and enjoying the bountiful fishing in the many small rivers that ended in the bay. Huge middens—piles of discarded clam shells often uncovered by shifting dunes—attest to the Indians' fondness for the easily obtained clams that were abundant in the mudflats of the barrier beaches. In 1616 Captain John Smith, on a mapping expedition along the coast of Massachusetts, described this area and its people:

Figure 3 This drawing depicts a typical Algonquin village.

> . . . the country of the Massachusetts which is the
> Paradise of all these parts. For heere are many isles
> all planted with corn; groves, mulberries, salvage
> gardens and good harbours . . . The Sea Coast as
> you pass, shews you all along large corn fields and
> great troops of well proportioned people.

The same year John Smith wrote so impres-
sively about the coastal Indians was the year
of the first great plague. In 1616 a pestilence
swept across New England, brought by the
European traders, and ultimately killed 80
percent of the Indian population. Most of the
Algonquin-speaking tribes which inhabited
the coast were affected; death songs were sung
by the campfires up and down the coastline,
from Virginia to New Hampshire. The white
traders and explorers who lived with some of
the Indians were untouched by the disease. It
might have been some kind of influenza, or
more likely, infectious hepatitis, for the bodies
of the dying turned quite yellow in the latter
course of the disease. The Indians had no resist-
ance to it and entire tribes were lost. In most
villages there were not enough healthy individ-
uals left to bury the dead.

Several smaller plagues succeeded the 1616
sickness; smallpox, influenza and starvation,
caused by the abandonment of fertile fields,
were the final blows. Later, the colonists instigated a program of burning whatever fields

they could find in an effort to starve out the remaining Indians. In the 1670s the Indians made a last great effort to retain their cultural integrity in New England during the King Phillip wars, but for all practical purposes the great homogeneous Algonquin culture of New England was broken, leaving only bits and shards of a once dynamic and spirited people.

In 1634, Masconomet, chief of the peaceful fishing tribe of the Agawams, leading only a few pitiful remnants of his beloved people, voluntarily submitted to the jurisdiction of the Massachusetts Colony government.

This tale is told over and over again, not only in New England, but all along the Atlantic coast, wherever the early explorers and traders interacted with the coastal Indians. The demise of these Indians was so sudden and catastrophic that little knowledge of their extensive culture and trade has survived. However, that they greatly helped the early colonists, and even passed on to them parts of their culture that proved invaluable to the future of the entire coastline, cannot be denied.

The early colonists had to depend upon the Indians as trading partners to obtain furs and food in exchange for their guns, knives and cloth. But to the Indian a promissory note of payment, or even a piece of British sterling, was worthless. The early colonists had to adopt the Indian wampum as the *lingua franca* of trade. The wampum prized by the Indians of New England, which was traded up and down the coast all the way to Florida and north to Maine, was primarily found on Fire Island, along the shores of Great South Bay. Wampum is made from the purple spot found in the shells of the hard-shell clams. The purple section of the shell was carved into cylindrical beads about an eighth of an inch in diameter and a quarter of an inch long, and strung on leather thongs. In fact, the Indian's word for Fire Island—"Paumanauke"—means "Isle of

Tribute," showing its importance as a source of this early currency. For hundreds of years wampum was the great medium of exchange in the lucrative fur trade. The powerful confederacy of the Narragansett Indians of Connecticut exacted tribute in wampum from their vassals, the Long Island Indians. Both the Dutch and English traders accepted wampum as currency for their transactions with the Indians until the early 1800s.

Nantucket has a long and fascinating history in the whaling industry, but the art of capturing the whale did not originate there. The Indians of Long Island killed whales along the beach and taught the first white settlers how to do it—and launched the long and colorful history of the whaling industry in the United States. The Indians pursued the whales in dugout canoes, spearing them in open water or driving schools of whales to flounder upon the beach. Once stranded, the whales were dispatched, and the whole village would move down to the killing site and have a week-long celebration.

With his advanced technology and larger ships, the white man soon took over the whaling industry from the Indians. The fame of the Long Island whalers soon grew to such proportions that in 1672 the citizens of Nantucket invited one Captain Loper of Long Island to teach them how to capture and process whales.

From the Indians the colonists obtained what was to become the most important field crop in the world—corn—and the means to grow, fertilize and harvest it. Along with the corn the Indians added two other valuable crops, squash and beans. These crops originated in Mexico and Central America, but through the centuries the Indians cultivated different varieties that would grow in varying conditions along the Atlantic coastline. To survive the early colonists had to use the Indians' seeds, learn the technique of hill cultivation (a highly productive means of growing corn, beans and squash on the same small pile of soil—a practice unknown in Europe) and to use fish for fertilization.

Barrier beaches were used extensively to store surplus food. The Indians taught the colonists the secret of digging large pits in the sand and lining them with bark or clay. In the arid conditions of the sand, food would keep all winter.

For many ships traversing the ocean during those early times, a barrier beach was the first glimpse of the new world. This was so for Colonel Henry Norwood on January 3, 1650. He led a small party of women and men who had been put ashore to find supplies and a safe harbor on Assateague Island. The ship was bound for the Virginia colony from England by way of the West Indies. The party found plenty of birds to shoot and fresh water, but the next morning the ship inexplicably sailed without them. Put to their own resources, and not having much knowledge of woodcraft or survival skills, they endured frostbite, sickness and starvation, and finally had to resort to cannabalism to survive. With only a handful of the party left, some local Indians found them, gave them food, taught them some basic survival techniques, and gave them safe passage on to the Virginia colony.

This story of hardship by the colonists and rescue by the Indians is all too familiar in the history of the coastal areas. Except for an occasional arrowhead or clam shell midden found among the dunes, there is almost nothing left behind by these Indians to further our knowledge of them. The early colonists villified the Indians, calling them savages and godless people. Even though they had benefited from their food and adaptive technology, many early colonial societies, especially those that were Puritan, instigated policies of harassment, torture and murder to rid themselves of a race of people they regarded as no better than their dogs. What has been forgotten is the great integrity of the Indian as a people. The English tried for decades to develop a slave trade, shipping hundreds of Indians back to Europe, but to no avail. The Indians valued their liberty above all else—most Indian slaves killed themselves (or were killed trying to escape) before they could ever be put to work.

The colonists were so busy eradicating the Indians they didn't have any motivation to study their culture. What does remain are the place names from their expressive Algonquin language: Assateague and Chincoteague, Nanticoke and Pocomoke, Massachusetts and Connecticut, Agawam and Merrimack, Ocracoke and Roanoke.

The Lay of the Land

Some 2,500 years ago the citizens of Carthage, a Phoenician people, built a harbor along the shores of the Gulf of Tunis in North Africa. This harbor, from which Hannibal sailed to attack Rome, is still used today by small Arab fishing boats.

A few hundred years later and some twenty miles away, the Romans, a mightier people, built the seaport of Utica. North Africa was the breadbasket of the Roman Empire, and across the docks of Utica flowed huge quantities of food and treasure to be shipped to the motherland. Today, a tourist standing atop the highest column in the ruins of Utica can no longer see the sea. The shoreline has moved 17 kilometers seaward, away from what once was the harbor.

The Carthaginians were careful to design to live with nature. The Romans, the first practitioners of brute-force technology, chose to confront, alter, and destroy nature. What the Romans didn't realize was that in the long run, nature always wins at the shoreline. (From *Currituck to Calabash,* the Introduction).

Even after 2,500 years, and technological advancements that would have made us gods to these ancients minds, the world, it seems, can still be divided into the Romans and the Carthaginians. At least the ancients can be forgiven because they lacked the science to fully understand the consequence of their actions. It would seem that we modern Romans don't have any excuse for our mismanagement of the coastline. But actually the study of the coastline, and of barrier beaches in particular, is a relatively new science, and much has yet to be learned before we can completely comprehend the complex and intricate landforms created when sand is moved around by the powerful forces of water and wind.

Barrier beach formation is based on certain simple, physical principles; somehow sand is dumped along the shore and wave and wind action picks the sand up and deposits it in a strip along the coast. This sounds simple enough, but the actual processes involved are extremely complex. Scientists are digging deep inside their bag of tricks and are using analytical devices like wave and particle physics and fluid dynamics as tools to reveal the secrets of beach and dune development. However, most investigations into the principles behind the formation of barrier beaches can be laid at the doorstep of geology, for it is the past 15,000 years of geological history that are mostly responsible for the coastal development along the Atlantic coastline.

The Atlantic coast that we are investigating can be divided neatly into two distinct regions: the New England coast (north of Long Island, New York, to southern Maine) and the Middle Atlantic coast (from Sandy Neck, New Jersey, to Cape Lookout, North Carolina). The barrier beaches along the New England coast were formed from the moraine deposits of the last glacial period and will be referred to as the glaciated coast. The barrier beaches along the Middle Atlantic coast, while affected by the rise and fall of sea level caused by the glaciers, have been more directly influenced by eroding headlands and the deposition created by large rivers. This area is the non-glaciated coast.

The Glaciated Coast

Eighteen thousand years ago a glacier a mile high covered much of North America, from the coast of Labrador to Long Island in New York. This glacier represented only the latest in a long series of glaciations going back about two million years. Since then, there have been about sixteen glacier periods of varying severity and extent, the last being named the Wisconsin period.

The tremendous weight of the glacier depressed the earth's crust until the sea level was about 600 feet below the present coastline. The coastline was 40 miles further east than the coastline of today. When the glaciers started to melt, they produced tremendous streams flowing along the edge of the melting ice sheet, combining and interlacing to form a broad wet plain in front of the glaciers, very similar to the tundra of northern Canada today. The climate was Wagnerian: the average temperature was around 40°F, with violent winds and eternal snowstorms.

When the glacier began its last retreat, about 15,000 years ago, it left behind great piles of rubble, called moraine material. Since the leading edge of the glacier was at least 40 miles east of the present coastline, a substantial amount of moraine material was deposited offshore, and glacier streams added enormous quantities of sand and gravel along the shoreline. If you look at a map of almost any barrier beach north of Long Island, New York, you will see the outlines of some of this outwashed glacial debris as large submerged sandbars that form the ocean floor close to the shore. Initially a mixture of gravel and sand from the glacier, this material is continuously reduced and suspended by the workings of the sea, which brings great quantities of it closer to shore, especially during storms.

As the great ice sheets retreated, two simultaneous effects resulted: the sea slowly began to rise as it filled with melted glacial water, and the earth's crust rebounded from the relief of the tremendous weight of the glaciers. These effects did not always happen at the same time, and the relationship between sea level and the rebounding land changed continuously. Sometimes the sea would rise faster than the land would rebound, flooding the existing coast and producing new inlets and coves. Sometimes the opposite would be the case, and a huge floodplain with great rivers and bays would form. These great, if short-lived, rivers cut into the moraine deposits along the coast and deposited them as river delta materials, scattering sand even further up and down the coast. Eventually, about 4,000 years ago, the rising sea and the still rising land stabilized into the contemporary coastline. The sea is still slowly rising, however, currently about six inches a century.

Around Long Island the glaciers came to a slow, thundering halt, and remained there, stagnant and rotting, for hundreds of years. Great rivers raced and churned from this decaying wall of ice, carrying enormous amounts of glacial till and debris and depositing it in great fan-shaped masses of rock, silt and sand. These outwash fans, as these deposits are called, piled layer upon layer of debris into broad flat plateaus, sometimes several hundred feet thick. Long undulating rows of these outwash fans form the foundation for many of the most prominent features of the glaciated coastline: Long Island, Block Island, Martha's Vineyard, Nantucket, and a great part of Cape Cod. Actually, there were at least two stages to the final recession of the glacier, and each recession left behind a long row of outwash moraine material. The moraine farthest west, called the Harbor Hill Moraine, forms part of the backbone of Long Island, nicks Rhode Island, bulges out beyond Buzzards Bay, and finally plays out beyond Cape Cod, forming the foundation for the lower part of the Cape. The Ronkonkora Moraine also starts at Long Island and parallels the coast farther east, forming the eastern highlands of Long Island and Block Island and swinging out to sea to create Martha's Vineyard and Nantucket before burying itself into the Atlantic.

Between Cape Cod, Massachusetts and Cape Elizabeth, Maine, the coast becomes a mixture of pocket beaches with soft, sandy headlands, becoming increasingly rocky the farther north you go. Here the geology is more complex, because we have entered the geological dividing line between the spectacular rockbound North Atlantic coast, and the pocket beaches and long barrier beaches characteristic of the more southern coastal development. This transition area has characteristics of both kinds of coasts, with the Cape Ann area of Massachusetts containing many long beautiful barrier beaches alongside promontories of rocky headlands.

A major contribution to the formation of barrier beaches along this coast are drumlins—low, dome-shaped hills caused by large amounts of debris rolled under the passing glaciers. Drumlins have a characteristic shape, described as an upturned spoon with the higher, rounder part almost always pointing east. A classic example of a drumlin-formed barrier beach is Plum Island, Massachusetts, where there are three drumlins—Cross-Farm Hill, Stage Island, and Bar Head. After the sea level stabilized, these drumlins were left as low, isolated islands off the coast. The ocean currents began to deposit the offshore moraine material as a sand spit that started around Boar's Head off the coast of New Hampshire and spread south to what is now Salisbury Beach. The beach kept lengthening, helped along by deposition from the Merrimack, Parker, and Ipswich rivers, and probably would have eventually strung itself out in an ever-thinning sand spit to disappear into the ocean, if it hadn't met the drumlins to the south.

Sand piled up on the first drumlin broadside, forming a mini-beach before becoming a moving spit again and eventually dribbling out to the next drumlin farther south. This process continued to build and thicken the line of sand until all the drumlins were connected. It was in this way that the basic dimension of Plum Island evolved. Once all the drumlins were connected and a barrier beach formed, a protected area, or sound, was created between it and the mainland. Protected from the harsh forces of the surf, an estuary developed, and a fresh water marsh began to grow along the edges of the mainland and the western edge of the new barrier beach. An extensive marsh soon developed, protecting the coastline between the barrier beach and the mainland. This fresh water marsh was eventually replaced by the present salt water marsh complex. In only a few hundred years, a barrier beach was formed that ran from the mouth of the Merrimack River to Ipswich Bay. But the same forces that created Plum Island, Crane's Beach, and other barrier beaches in the Cape Ann area, are still at work today—the coastal ocean currents move the sand like a conveyor belt from north to south, with the drumlins anchoring the whole dynamic process; they keep the barrier beach from becoming a sand spit that would, without support, soon play itself out into the ocean.

The Non-Glaciated Coast

The non-glaciated coastline was not covered by the immense glaciers, but that does not mean it was not greatly affected by their actions. One of the basic principles of barrier beach development is that there must be a broad, sloping coastal plain behind the developing beach. The Atlantic Coastal Plain becomes prominent just south of Cape Cod and extends down to Florida. This broad, relatively flat plain was formed during the Mesozoic era, approximately 70 million years ago, when the sea level was several hundred feet higher than it is today. For several million years the sea lapped against the foothills of the Appalacians. The foundation of what was to become Washington, D.C., and Norfolk, Virginia was built from several hundred feet of marine deposits buried under what was then the ocean. For eons the sea deposited layer upon layer of sediment and when the ice ages began in earnest, about 2 million years ago, the sea level dropped rapidly, exposing a broad, gently sloping plain. The dividing line between the earlier Mesozoic coastline and the modern coastline can be traced by the route of Interstate 95, which generally follows this geologic dividing line.

The substrate created by the slow accumulation of marine deposits is relatively soft and is quickly eroded. Coastal rivers cut easily into this soft material, and the James, Potomac and Roanoke rivers of the Middle Atlantic coast carry a much greater burden of sediment out to sea than the rivers of the glaciated coast, which flow over bedrock scraped clean by the recent glaciers. It is the sediment carried to sea by the slow moving rivers of the coastal plain that provides the basic building material of the barrier beaches of the middle Atlantic coast.

As long as the natural forces that affect the buildup of sand along the coast are left to their own devices, barrier beaches remain in a state of dynamic equilibrium. Although storms may momentarily destroy a section of dunes, or breach a low area to create a new inlet, these effects are transient. Eventually another storm may close the inlet or open another one, or shift the sand to a different point up or down the barrier beach. But man has dammed most of the rivers along the Middle Atlantic coast, slowing the rate of sedimentation that is the basic building material for these beaches. Combined with a recent rise in sea level, the choking of the sand supply to the coast by damming the rivers has resulted in overall widespread erosion along the coast. We are losing parts of the Outer Banks at the rate of 20 feet per year. And our modern technical skills in building huge groins or spending millions of dollars to pump sand back onto the beach have met with failure. By ignoring the integrity of the dynamic equilibrium necessary for the health of barrier beaches, we perpetuate our lack of intelligence and morality in dealing with the forces of nature.

Perhaps the Carthaginians had no choice but to live with the forces of nature and shaped their lives to this fact; they lacked the technology to do anything else. And yet, if the Romans can be accused of an excess of hubris in dealing with nature, then we should be similarly accused; developers seem to have more of a voice in the future of barrier beaches than do coastal scientists. We must become more Carthaginian than Roman in our attitudes toward barrier beaches if they are to survive.

The Dynamic Equilibrium

Walking the dunes I rise up and down among them like a small boat riding the ocean's waves. After a particularly long tramp my legs feel heavy, for walking long distances in loose sand is hard work. I stand at the top of a primary dune and sight along it to the horizon, toward the south where the beach curves gently eastward and out beyond my vision. It is high tide and great breakers are crashing to my left, running far up the beach and leaving thin lines of sand and debris that filigree the base of the dunes. The tall seed heads of the beach grass bow to the fierce wind. Blasts of sand streaming across the beach smash against the dunes.

Waves everywhere, wet and dry. The physics of wave energy I understand well. Energy moves *through* the water as waves, like a shiver across the thin skin of the sea, or like electricity through a copper wire. The wave eventually approaches land where the friction of the coastal bottom drags at the lower end of the wave, slowing it down, while the top part of the wave keeps going, shearing off from itself and spilling onto the beach. The release of energy is perceived as sound (the crashing of the surf) and the kinetic force of the wave carries sand and various bits of debris with it as it spends itself upon the beach. On an average of 8,000 times a day waves die upon the beach, each wave carrying a tiny load of sand particles and depositing it in its final act before finally shrinking back into the ocean.

I look from the beach to the dunes and I see more waves, except these aren't moving, at least not at a speed that I can perceive. These "solid" waves are derived, in some small way, from the spent energy of the ocean wave as it flops onto the beach and subsequently drops its load of sand. So the ocean waves deliver the sands which are sculptured into another type of wave form . . . by what? The wind? Of course, the wind ties the whole thing together. Somewhere in the Atlantic storms or strong winds eternally blow across the waters and create waves. These waves travel great distances almost undiminished in energy until they crash onto the beach. The sand on the beach is now picked up by the wind and bounced up the beach. This sorts out the sand grains according to their overall size and weight. Any obstruction along the beach, even the tiniest speck of wood or bit of shell, acts to trap sand into a tiny sand wave, that may join into a mound, that may, with time, coalesce into a dune.

As stated earlier, sand transport and barrier beach development are simple enough in principle, but each barrier beach is a unique expression of these principles. If you set up a movie camera to view a panorama of a barrier beach and took one frame a day for a year and then ran it back at a fast speed, you would see the beach rise and fall, broaden and narrow according to the season. During the replay you would notice that through the seasons the beach responds with a measured regularity except at certain times, when suddenly the beach drops several feet and its whole profile radically changes. These are storms, hurricanes or northeasters, that can, in a few hours, affect as much change in the beach profile as many months or years of normal seasonal wear.

If you reset the camera to take one picture a month for 100 years and then replayed the movie, you would notice the dunes themselves begin to move. A dune ridge moves like a monstrous slug, slowly burying everything in its path. Several smaller dunes may elongate and join together, spreading like an organic growth in a Petri dish. You would also notice changes along the primary dunes, the ridge of dunes that faces the beach. Large gaps would suddenly appear; the dune ridge would be blasted away as if it were blown up with dynamite, and the loose sand pushed far inland, burying the interior vegetation. Then you would see the

loose sand piled up in a low dune ridge, or perhaps several smaller dunes, which may eventually build into a larger dune complex several
hundred feet landward of the original blasted
primary dune.

As the movie played on you would notice this
happening over and over again up and down
the edge of the dunes. By the end of 100 years
you could come to only one conclusion: the
whole beach complex moving landward was
caused by a series of storms that punched out
holes in the dunes, pushing the blasted sand
inward to create another line of dunes farther
back. And you would notice one other unset-
tling thing: the sea level was definitely rising,
causing a slow, inexorable creep of the sea upon
the land—600 feet in 10,000 years. That's
about fifty miles of shore eaten up since the
last glaciers rumbled back to Greenland. The
rising sea level has not happened in one steady
climb, but in fits and starts through recent
history. Scientists have noticed that since the
middle of this century the rise in sea level has
definitely accelerated, and it may be as much
as a foot a century for some locations along the
northeast coast. Nobody knows for sure why
the rise in sea level has accelerated since the
1940s. The Greenhouse Effect could be one
explanation, leading to higher overall surface
temperatures and subsequent melting of the
polar ice caps. These higher average global
temperatures could produce as much as a six-
foot rise in the next century, which would be
disastrous for major cities located in low-lying
coastal areas.

Scientists have discovered that the north and
south polar regions are dotted with tiny flecks
of soot. This soot originates from industrial
complexes in the Midwest, Russia and Western
Europe. The soot absorbs the sun's heat, which
could contribute to a higher melt rate of the
polar ice caps.

The rising sea level is the primary driving force behind the retreat of the beach toward the mainland. The dynamics of a barrier beach literally rolling over upon itself and migrating toward the mainland can't happen without a rising sea level. Indeed, if the sea level were static or lowering, the reverse would be the case; the beaches would be growing outward at a pace in proportion to the amount of the lowering of the sea level. This happened in the distant past, after the last ice age, when the earth's surface rebounded faster than the sea level rose from the melting glaciers. Many barrier beaches were formed several miles eastward of their present location and have retreated to their present site by this "rolling over" process.

If we next tied our camera with a wide angle lens to the top of a pole 500 feet high, our view would encompass the ocean, the barrier beach, the salt marsh that forms the edge of the barrier beach, and the protected sound behind it. Taking a picture a month for 500 years and playing it back like a movie would offer a truly astounding scene. Not only does the beach itself flex and shift, but the ocean, the salt marsh and the sound changes dramatically. Sand bars form and disappear in an instant along the shore, seeming to march right up to the beach and attaching themselves as "berms"—humps of sand deposited at the edge of the high tide line. Sand from these berms is blown up the beach and becomes the source of sand for development of the primary dunes. We see definite patterns in the movement of the dunes as several smaller dunes flow together and form a dune ridge, which may eventually bury a small tract of pitch pine or loblolly pine. Some dunes attain a favorable position, become heavily vegetated, are stabilized, and are passed on by its neighbors still on the move. Dune ridges grow together and split apart, whole areas are flattened repeatedly only to grow back again, and inlets form and are filled in.

Within this broad time frame we can discern changes in the salt marsh that rings the western edge of the barrier beach. Violent storms wash out large sections of the primary dunes, bulldozing large amounts of sand across the interior dunes and burying acres of beach grass and shrubs. Through this open wound strong winds blow enormous quantities of sand from the beach to the low-lying salt marsh. Over the years the western edge of the island gradually widens because of this deposition; the salt marsh grows westward, generally compensating for the gradual westward creep of the beach. Sometimes, at narrow sections of the barrier beach, a washout will spill over the entire barrier beach and sand will be deposited directly onto the salt marsh. This section of the marsh develops quickly, and it soon becomes a small saltmarsh peninsula with several tidal creeks meandering through it.

The shallow sound behind the barrier beach gradually narrows. As long as the sea level steadily rises, the barrier beach slowly moves toward the mainland. Eventually, after a thousand years or more, it merges with the mainland, and the barrier beach is no more.

Figure 4 Overwash, where storm waves wash over weak sections of the primary dunes, is a fundamental process of barrier beach dynamics. Here an overwash has pushed sand into the interior behind the dunes and on-shore winds have continued to blow sand over the vegetation.

The barrier beach doesn't *have* to merge with the coast. Before it even gets close to the coast it might elongate into an ever-thinning spit. It might get so thin that it gets breached repeatedly in storms, becoming a tattered line of smaller beaches and inlets. If it is a New England barrier beach it may become a series of small islands, perhaps just a series of drumlins, each one ringed by a tiny beach. Farther south the low, narrow barrier beach sites may become a series of low, broken islands called *cheniers,* standing just a few inches above the water and thickly covered with live oak and holly trees. Eventually, all barrier beaches, no matter where they are located, will be drastically altered by the rising sea level and the forces of sea and wind.

How Barrier Beaches are Formed

Barrier beaches are difficult to study because their formation is the result of a complex and subtle series of geomorphic principles. Much of the science of geology is based on certain theories that are accepted for the moment, and the study of barrier beaches is no exception. Currently there are three main theories of barrier beach genesis: upbuilding of submarine bars (the deBeaumont-Johnson theory); spit growth and segmentation by inlets (the Gilbert-Fisher theory); and mainland beach ridge submergence (the Hoyt theory). It is generally accepted that most barrier beaches are the result of a combination of each of these three theories, although one theory may dominate in the development of a barrier beach, depending upon its location along the coastline.

Most of the barrier beaches of the New England area are formed according to the spit accretion theory. Sand is furnished either by headlands, an eroding drumlin, or offshore sand deposits from the last glaciation. Ocean currents sweep the coast in a north-to-south direction, depositing the sand in a spit that gradually elongates into a fingerlike ridge that is attached to the mainland but ends in the open ocean or a bay. A sound is formed behind the barrier beach and an extensive salt marsh may grow in the estuary. Plum Island, Crane's Beach, Fire Island, Monomoy Island, and Nauset Beach are some examples of barrier beaches along the North Atlantic coastline that were probably formed according to the spit accretion theory.

Barrier beaches of the mid-Atlantic coastline are thought to be formed by different means than those of the Northeast coast. Here the tides are not so extreme and the development of barrier beaches is more subtle and complex. Hoyt's theory of barrier beach formation—by drowning of a mainland dune ridge—may answer some of the complexities of barrier formation in this area. As the sea level rose, dune ridges along the coast were drowned, becoming isolated, elongated beaches surrounded by water. Ocean currents and waves continued to shape them into their present form.

Even though there are several theories of barrier beach development, the basic principles of dynamic equilibrium affects them all in one way or another. By dynamic equilibrium I mean the system of *energies* that affects the sand, not individual sand grains and their eventual formations. These energies come from two elements: water and wind. But strangely enough, even the energies that drive the water into waves which moves the sand ultimately comes from the wind, for it's the wind's energy that originally makes the waves. So it's that invisible energy source, the wind, that is the ultimate progenitor of the entire system. Without the interplay of the wind and the sea to produce the waves no sand would be thrown upon the beach; without the rush of the wind no sand would be blown across the beach to form the dunes.

Water-Borne Sand

Once sand is brought close to shore by wave action it is affected by the *Longshore Currents*, and *Beach Drift*. Longshore currents are caused by waves arriving at an angle to the shore. When a wave nears the shore, the lower part of it drags on the ocean bottom. This slows that section of the wave, turning it so that it is more parallel to the shore. The entire wave is deformed from a straight wave to a curved one; the end of the wave closest to shore slows down while the rest of the wave continues at its original speed until it too enters the shallow area. This disparity of energies approaching the coast creates a current that flows in the direction of the refracted waves. This Longshore Current is responsible for transporting huge amounts of sand along the coast, and with moving the bulk of the sand brought up to the beach by wave action along the coastline. Along the Atlantic coast it generally moves from north to south. If you look at the map located in the inside back cover of this book you will notice that almost all the barrier beaches are built from sand moved by a north-to-south longshore current. Much of the long-distance movement of sand along a beach is caused by the longshore currents. A grain of sand from Cape Hatteras might have originated from the southern coast of Maine.

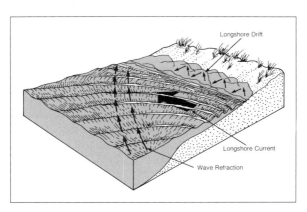

Figure 5 This figure illustrates three important beach dynamic principles. *Wave Refraction* happens when ocean waves are bent as they approach the coast. The *Longshore Currents* move sand generally in a north-to-south direction along the beach. *Longshore Drift* moves sand in a zig-zag fashion down the beach when waves drop their load of sand.

As the longshore current shunts huge quantities of sand along the beach, the surf carries the sand up to the beach. The turbulent area of the surf zone keeps huge quantities of sand in eternal suspension. Every time a wave flops upon the beach it carries with it a load of sand. But no wave ever breaks perfectly parallel to the shore and consequently the wave flows up the beach at an angle. Gravity causes the wave to flow pretty much straight back into the surf zone. The suspended sand is picked up by the next wave coming in at a slight angle and moved up the beach again. The result is a zig-zag motion of the sand grains as they are deposited along the beach. This staggered sand deposition is called *beach or longshore drifting.* The marks of this deposition can easily be seen at low tide. The lower beach will be filigreed with the swash marks of the waves as they tumble up the beach pushing their load of sand at the very tip of the wave. Friction and gravity soon overcome the energy of the wave, and at its apogee it releases the sand and sighs back into the surf zone, leaving a swash of sand as a result of its work.

Eight to twelve thousand times a day waves pass over the beach, each one adding its tiny layer of sand on top of the previous wave. A beach is really made up of millions of thin sand layers. How much sand is actually deposited by each wave is ultimately determined by the season. In summer, waves tend to be smaller and spaced farther apart. They leave more sand behind on their surge up the beach than they drag back down to the surf zone during the backwash. Sand tends to build up during the summer months, creating a beach that is broad and level. During winter there are more storms, and the average wave is higher and more closely spaced, so these winter waves take more sand into the surf zone on the backwash than they leave on the beach during the initial surge. By spring quite a bit of sand has been moved from the beach to the shoals in the surf zone, creating a beach that is much steeper and narrower than its summer version. Over several seasons the balance between sand loss and sand gain is maintained, another illustration of the theory of dynamic equilibrium.

Barrier beaches "store" sand in various forms. Offshore bars are a form of stored sand that is in equilibrium with the ocean waves and currents until something happens to disrupt that equilibrium—seasonal changes in wave height and frequency may start to move sand from the bar toward the shore, or a storm may suddenly remove great quantities of it in a single day. The mound of sand deposited at the high tide line, called the "berm," is another example of stored sand. This is really a "dry" sand bar that has been moved up the beach by the action of the swash of waves. This berm contains dry sand except at high tide or during storms, when it may disappear altogether, only to reappear as a bar a short distance offshore. Once the sand is deposited on the beach the wind takes over the job of moving the sand.

Wind-Borne Sand

Strong winds are common on barrier beaches. Barrier beaches and barrier islands usually bear the brunt of the wind because they present a low profile to the weather and because of their vulnerable position, lying with the ocean on one side and a broad sound on the other. If it's windy on the mainland, it's really blowing on the beach!

Windy days move sand around, but how much sand is moved depends on the wind speed and the duration of the blow. A light breeze will move only the very lightest and smallest particles. They will only eddy around in a circular fashion, not moving very far from their origin. It takes winds of around 30 mph to begin to pick up quantities of sand. At this velocity the sand is plucked from the beach, carried a short distance and dropped. When the sand particle hits the beach surface, the impact throws up several other sand particles which are in turn

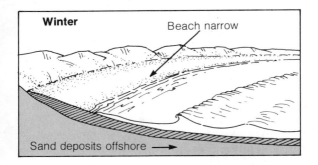

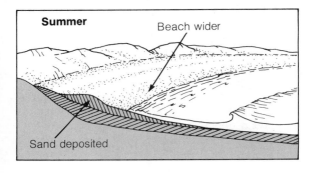

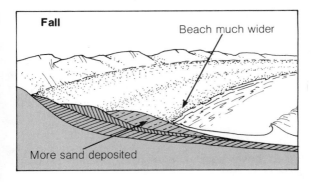

Figure 6 Seasonal changes in the amplitude and frequency of ocean waves affect the profile of a beach.

picked up by the wind and carried a few feet and then dropped. The process continues as long as the wind velocity is great enough to pick up sand particles; sand is picked up and dropped, and more particles are rebounded by the impact and picked up by the wind. If the wind is strong enough, sand particles by the billion are moved across the beach, bouncing and banging together, looking exactly like someone shaking salt on a table top. In fact, the process is called *saltation*.

An Examination of Sand

Sand is not uniform in size or shape. If you pick up a handful of sand you will see that it is made up of many colors and shapes. Each color generally represents a different mineral that constitutes a typical handful of sand. The black particles are usually magnetite, and can be tested by passing a magnet over the sand; the black particles will adhere to the magnet. Red particles are usually garnet, a semi-precious gem. But the vast majority of particles will be quartz, a very hard, light-colored mineral that represents the final reduction of millions of years of being weathered and ground together during the various ice ages.

During storms, the sand particles are sorted out by the wind and the surf; the heaviest minerals fall first, collecting around the base of established dunes or dumped in specific areas during the backwash. The slightly lighter quartz particles are pushed further inland, with the finest particles carried far into the interior of the barrier beach by the wind. This sorting of heaviest to lightest particles can easily be observed on the beach. Look for areas of red or black-colored sand; here surf sorted out the heaviest particles and dumped them in a particular spot. A graphic example of wind-sorted sand can be seen on slopes; the larger sand grains, or the heaviest sand particles, will be at the bottom of the slope, and the smaller, lighter grains, will be at the top.

The composition of sand varies greatly with
location. Barrier beaches along the New England coast down to New Jersey have sand that
is a mixture of quartz, magnetite, lignite and
garnet. After a storm it is common to find these
beaches patterned with swashes of red and
black against the light quartz sand. The
beaches of the mid-Atlantic coast contain sand
that is almost entirely quartz, with a large
part of the sand composed of shell fragments.
The percentage of shell fragments increases as
you travel south until, reaching the beaches of
Florida, you will find the beaches almost entirely made of shell fragments with very
little quartz.

Primary Dune Formation

Sand dunes are formed by the slow build-up of
sand around obstacles—no matter whether
those obstacles are beach grass, other dune
vegetation, or even old clam shell mounds left
from the days when the coastal Indians used
the barrier beach as a summer home.

The dunes right by the beach, called primary
dunes, are usually formed by obstacles on the
upper beach, beyond the strand line. These
obstacles create mini-dunes that act as "seed"
areas, building up and coalescing until larger
dunes are created. These can be formed by
colonies of beach grass, old clam shell mounds,
piles of refuse, a mound of heavier sand particles, or even a ship's beam washed ashore during a storm. Given the right conditions, just
about any obstacle can form the foundation for
a primary dune, as long as it retains the sand
long enough for the building process to begin.
You will see examples of this as you walk along
the upper beach; watch for old sections of trees,
ship timbers, clam mounds, fish netting, or
darker foundations of heavier sand particles
that have been exposed during weathering.

Like old sculpture left in the sand, these old
dune foundations are often exposed after a
dune has eroded away, perhaps to start another
dune if the conditions permit.

Storms

It is during storms that the principles of the dynamic equilibrium are most visible. The normal actions of the sea upon the beach are speeded up hundreds of times until as much sand is moved during the few hours of a typical storm as could be moved in a few years of calmer weather. Powerful storms with winds generally from the northeast periodically slam into the northeast coast, sometimes causing as much damage as a hurricane. Hurricanes are more frequent along the middle Atlantic coast and several of these storms—which pack a wallop as big as several atomic bombs—devastate coastal areas every decade. Storms release tremendous amounts of energy from the atmosphere onto the surface of the earth and the whole structure of the beach is altered as a response to this great venting of the earth's energy. The storm focuses the energy of several months or years of weather into a single day and the beach responds by yielding itself to the force, a kind of Zen of beach maintenance.

A single northeast storm can move as much sand in a few hours as the lighter prevailing winds have moved all year. For example, one hour of wind blowing at 50 mph will move as much sand as when the wind blows 30 mph for 14.3 hours. At 20 mph it takes 611 hours to move as much sand as is moved in 1 hour at 50 mph! It becomes apparent that the direction of the storm winds is usually more important in the dynamics of barrier beaches than the direction of the prevailing winds.

Like China before the invading hordes, the beach retreats before the storm, but at the same time it absorbs the storm's energy. Berms flatten as the waves surge up the beach, and the primary dunes bear the brunt of the relentless wind. Sand is torn off the dunes and flung inland across the salt marshes. Every grain of sand that is moved during a storm takes away some of the storm's energy. A barrier beach could be perceived as a huge buffer, which flexes and shifts from the body blows of the storm. On the other side of the barrier beach the mainland is spared the ravages of the storm. The sound behind the beach may become choppy, but it certainly doesn't have the terrible force of the storm-lashed ocean.

How Storms Help Create Interior Dunes

A northeasterly storm probes at any weak section of the primary dunes; it works and worries a dune like a wolf seeking a weakness in its prey. There may be a section of dune that isn't well bound by the beach grass, so strong winds may gouge out a notch that may evolve, during the course of the storm, into a split in the dune. A dune may also be cut in half by the driven surf, but once a weakness is found and the dune breached—either by powerful surf surges or by the cutting effect of the sand-laden wind—the dune is soon transformed. The storm turns a weakness into a wound, and an ever-widening gap is cut into the dune.

During a storm surge, sand-loaded water flows over this gap like a thick, viscous fluid which buries beach grass and other dune plants under several inches of sand. This sand and other debris (old tires, chunks of salt marsh sod, bottles, bleach containers, aerosol cans, etc.) is called an *overwash*. The overwash flows around

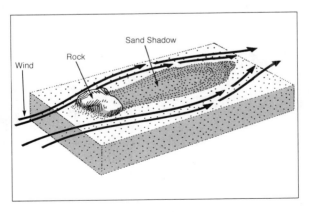

Figure 7 Even the smallest obstacle can create conditions which may later lead to the development of a sand dune.

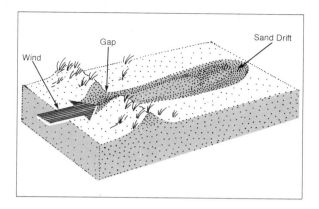

Figure 8 "Blowouts" happen when wind scours out an ever-widening gap in the dunes.

and between the dunes, often creating a fan-shaped area of sand and rubble. The storm surge pushes the sand ahead of it like a bulldozer, and, when the storm abates, it leaves behind a low ridge of sand and debris at the head of the overwash.

The storm surge creates two conditions that promote sand movement into the interior: a gap in the primary dunes that gives strong easterly winds an unobstructed path to the vulnerable interior, and a large expanse of exposed sand, stripped of its vegetation cover, left to the vagaries of the wind.

Strong winds, channeled by the gap in the dunes, begin to scour out a shallow trough in the overwash area. This wind-scoured trough, called a *blowout,* adds more sand to the low ridge at its head, which builds rapidly during the storm, sometimes as much as several feet. The gap in the primary dunes created by the overwash acts as a channel for sand movement, passing large quantities of sand from the beach, through the blowout and into the interior of the dunes. Eventually, during successive storms, the new ridge at the head of the blowout might mature into a dune ridge, adding to the strange and wonderful dune shapes found throughout the interior of a barrier beach.

A
Primary dunes absorb the energy of storms and protect
the interior of the barrier beach.

B
A powerful storm surge has breached the primary dunes.
The sand from the dunes is pushed into the interior,
creating the typical fan-shaped overwash. The overwash
buries beach vegetation under several inches of sand.

Figure 9 The sand and beach vegetation combine to heal
an overwash. The result is a new line of primary
dunes developing several yards farther inland.
These four panels represent about ten years of
beach activity.

C

Two years have elapsed since the storm. Other storms and strong winds have blown much sand through the opening of the primary dunes created by the overwash. A small sand ridge has built up at the head of the overwash, and new primary dunes are beginning to form several yards back from the original dune line.

D

After ten years the sand ridge has grown into a line of low dunes. The new primary dunes have become higher, and the whole complex has shifted inland somewhat. Vegetation has taken advantage of the protection now offered by the new primary dunes. Another storm may create an overwash at this location again, wiping out whatever dunes have formed and pushing large amounts of sand into the interior. Or an overwash might happen down the beach, leaving these dunes to continue to grow and shift for themselves.

The storm-ravaged primary dune, cut off from its neighbors and without support, rapidly erodes, its sand blown into the interior through the channel of the blowout. But new stands of beach grass move into these raw sand areas, and new dunes begin to form in back of the old primary dune. The rising sea has a part in all this too, rising on the average about 6 inches a century along the Atlantic coast. This gradually cuts back the beach, forcing the dunes to migrate slowly inland. In this way the barrier beach literally rolls over upon itself; the sand from the primary dunes is used to build dunes in the interior, and the interior dunes may eventually become the front-line primary dunes. And so the destruction of the old primary dune feeds a new dune behind it; and like a living thing, the barrier beach flexes and shifts, dies and is reborn.

Barrier Beach Migration

Many house lots just a few yards away from the high tide line are selling for $100,000 or more in the developed sections of barrier beaches. New owners of these modern houses sit in their glassed-in living rooms and sip cool drinks, feeling safe because their house is built on stilts and fits so snugly behind the primary dune that was bulldozed up just before the

Figure 10 This newly-constructed house sits precariously close to the primary dune. The next major storm will probably destroy it.

housing development was constructed. Just think, they can walk about 20 paces and there they are, sloshing their toes in the surf!

Beach walkers along these heavily developed shores, from New Jersey to the Outer Banks, are often puzzled by the sudden appearance after storms of thick, fibrous black mats of vegetation sticking out of the beach in the surf zone. Sometimes you can make out the remnants of tree stumps, complete with buttressed roots, grasping the black mats like the talons of a giant, extinct bird. These are the remains of peat beds and relict forests that once grew on the back side of the barrier beach. But how did they become repositioned to the front of the beach, and what happened to the once extensive pine or cedar forests that once grew there?

An area of the Outer Banks known as Currituck can be used to answer these questions. People have always had difficulty living on Currituck. In 1828 the sound behind Currituck silted in, and the result was a gradual increase of fresh water into the sound, destroying the shellfish industry of the area and forcing many people to move elsewhere for their livelihood. In the 1950s, a huge dune ridge some 75 feet high, called Penny's Hill, began to migrate toward the little fishing village of Sea Gull. By the early 1960s the sand had buried every remaining house in the village. In 1962 a great storm demolished the village of Penny Hill and washed over extensive areas of the barrier island. But, by the 1970s, developers were selling house lots on the very location that had been obliterated a few years before the storm.

Because sections of Currituck were slated to come under the auspices of the National Park Service, its dynamics were studied intensively during the late 1960s. One young botanist, Paul Godfrey from the University of Massachusetts, became interested in the origin of these peat deposits that kept appearing along the beach. For a summer he probed and tested various areas along Currituck's beach, taking many test core samples and analyzing the peat, bits of wood and pollen that were retrieved. From these samples he was able to piece together a sketchy anatomy of the barrier island, and to begin to unlock the mysteries of barrier beach migration.

Godfrey observed that the peat and stump deposits were actually remnants of marshes and maritime forests that grew along the *back* side of the barrier beach. The only way they could have possibly come to appear on the present beach is if the whole barrier beach complex literally rolled over upon itself, moving landward over a period of 500 to 1000 years. Five hundred years ago Currituck, complete with dunes and a maritime forest, was a mile east of its present location. Fifteen thousand years ago, he postulated, Currituck was 50 miles east of its present location!

Godfrey's work, with the help of other coastal scientists, has set the tone for modern understanding of dynamics of barrier beaches. Earlier concepts of barrier beach dynamics viewed stability as the desired goal for beach development. The primary dunes were considered to be most effective if they presented a solid wall

Figure 11 Remnants of a maritime forest that used to grow along the back side of Assateague Island, Maryland.

of sand to the ocean. Overwashes were promptly fenced off and sand bulldozed across the opening to plug the breach in the wall-like continuity of the dunes. Where barrier beaches were broken during storms, creating inlets, they were either fixed in place by building jetties at the mouth of the inlet to prevent the inlet from migrating, or millions of dollars were spent dredging sand to and fro to keep the inlet open. Developers ignored the previous history of storms and destruction along barrier beaches and built housing developments close to the beach, often constructing the houses on stilts situated behind bulldozed dunes.

Now we know that the overwash of primary dunes during storms is a vital process of the dynamic equilibrium of barrier beaches. Overwash allows sand to be shunted into the interior of the barrier beach, which builds the secondary dunes, providing shelter from the salt spray so that swales and maritime forests can develop. On some especially low and narrow barrier islands, such as those of the Outer Banks, overwash contributes greatly to the building of the salt marsh complex attached to the western part of the barrier beach. Setting the mouth of inlets with jetties, and building groin fields along the beach to restrict erosion, proves futile in the majority of cases. Inlets pass tremendous quantities of sand through the barrier beach to the sound, and they are the primary device for creating land in the sound behind the existing barrier beach, to which the beach is then appended. If left alone, inlets have a tendency to migrate along a barrier beach, spewing sand around like a giant slow-motion dredge. This sand builds up the back of the migrating barrier beach while the front is slowly eroded away by the rising sea level. In this way inlets provide a balance of sand to offset the natural erosion that takes place in all barrier beaches.

If the sea level were not rising, the various elements that produce barrier beach migra-

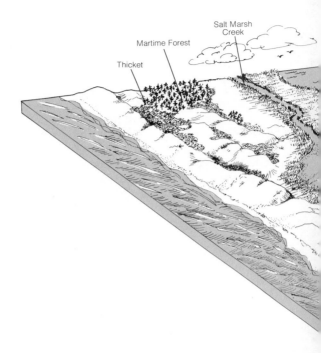

Salt Marsh
Creek

Martime Forest

Thicket

Figure 12 This overview drawing shows some major features of a typical barrier beach. Notice how the
height and proximity of the dunes determine
the extent of plant growth.

tion—overwash, inlet formation and longshore
currents—would keep the barrier beach in a
more-or-less stable condition. Approximately
as much sand would be added to the system by
accretion as is lost due to storms or currents.
The barrier beach would be in dynamic equilibrium to the sea. But because of the rising sea
level, the dynamic equilibrium turns into a
disequilibrium, with landward migration of
the barrier beach an inevitable result.

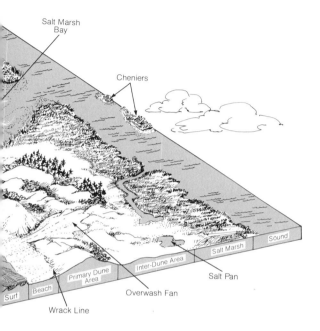

Salt Marsh Bay

Cheniers

Sound

Salt Marsh

Inter-Dune Area

Salt Pan

Primary Dune Area

Overwash Fan

Surf

Beach

Wrack Line

Plants of The Dunes

Dunes would constantly be formed and re-
formed, built up and torn down, without the
genius of certain plants to colonize such a
changeable environment. With no beach grass
or goldenrod, no beach pea or poison ivy,
storms would blow the sand freely, and the
dunes would be on a slow motion rampage,
marching back and forth across the barrier
beach at will.

While the moraine deposits of the last glacier
period and the ocean's longshore currents deposit the sand upon the beach, strong winds
push the sand inland and dune vegetation
traps the sand, thereby building the dunes.
Once some beach grass or poison ivy has
gained a foothold, the dune stops migrating
and begins the building process. When a dune
becomes heavily covered with beach grass or
other dune vegetation, the building process
slows down and the dune's shape is stabilized.

Dune vegetation has to deal with some of the
harshest environmental forces on the earth.
On a hot July day I have registered a tempera-

Figure 13 This interdune area on Fire Island National
Seashore is complex and relatively stable, due,
in part, to the healthy stands of beach grass,
beach heather, and other dune plants that can
grow in sand.

ture of 165°F on the sand's surface. Normal soil particles retain moisture, but sand particles are too large to trap much moisture, and water quickly percolates through the porous sand, out of reach of young shoots and unspecialized root systems.

Surface Micro-Climate

The first three inches from the sand's surface is a critical area that determines the suitability of a dune for pioneering vegetation. A dune's surface that is directly exposed to the wind leaves no opportunity for colonization. Sand grains are constantly blown about, quickly burying prospective seedlings. Those surfaces that are exposed to direct sunlight bake any life form that is unlucky enough to land in the vicinity. Life here is as extreme as a desert. From this tiny perspective, the sand's surface may as well be a desert planet, slowly baking in the sun.

But the appearance of beach grass or other dune vegetation changes the surface microclimate dramatically. It sets up the first of a series of complex changes that will produce a lush vegetation zone supporting a diversity of life forms. Even a single grass plant catches some sand. Look at a strand of beach grass and you'll see a tiny sand mound built up around its base. The temperature of this mound is slightly cooler than the sand around it, and this stimulates the grass plants to grow. The grass leaf shades the immediate area around the stem, further lowering the surface microclimate and making the environment beneath the grass more favorable for other forms of life.

Deserts and Dunes

Many plants that inhabit the dunes have evolved adaptive devices for survival similar to desert plants. Beach dunes and desert areas have some remarkably similar characteristics. Both lack water, but for very different reasons. A desert is characterized by hot, dry conditions, with very little rainfall. Consequently, most of the life forms living in a desert have evolved means to protect themselves against heat and desiccation. Sagebrush is a common plant in this arid environment which has evolved an extensive root system to obtain and store moisture. Its leaves and branches are covered with downy hairs that reflect the hot sun and insulate against moisture loss from its succulent parts.

Dune vegetation must also cope with extreme water shortages, but for different reasons. Although the ocean pounds the beach just yards away, the high salt content severely limits the kind of plant that can benefit directly from this water source. In fact, many plants must protect themselves from the ocean and the salt spray that it flings upon the dunes or they will die.

There is no shortage of fresh water either, for the average annual rainfall along coastal New England is about 39 inches (100 centimeters), but the topography of bare sand makes it difficult for any but the most specialized plants to benefit from a sand surface through which water percolates so quickly.

So dune ecology is characterized by conditions that are strikingly similar to a desert environment. And many of its plants cope with these conditions in a similar way. The dune counterpart of the desert sagebrush is Dusty Miller, which has evolved similar characteristics to adapt to hot, dry sand conditions. Its leaf surface is small compared to its overall size, and it has an extensive shallow root system that efficiently captures precious water as it percolates rapidly through the sand. But the most striking similarity is the fine, downy, silver hairs that cover the leaf and stems of both sagebrush and dusty miller. This downy coat protects against desiccation.

Some scientists believe the fine silver hairs also act as tiny mirrors, bouncing the sun's rays between them and reflecting them off into space.

Dune vegetation of New England barrier beaches must cope with an additional environmental extreme—arctic conditions. Heavy, wet snow sometimes burdens trees and shrubs until they break, especially evergreen species such as pitch pine. During winter storms, a mixture of sand and granular snow blasts the dune plants. While inland the dunes and back areas are covered with a protective layer of snow, the wind usually blows the snow off the primary dunes, depriving the vegetation of even this much protection. Below-freezing temperatures and high winds create bitterly cold conditions, adding more stress to vegetation that is already close to its limit of tolerance.

Figure 14 Snow cover protects plants from the sand blast of winter winds and insulates them from the bitter cold conditions prevalent on New England barrier beaches.

Many dune and desert plants use some of the techniques mentioned above as part of their repertoire for survival. Those plants that can use one or more of these techniques efficiently will not only survive, but are capable of flourishing among conditions that would kill other plants. For such a plant to endure, it must develop special modifications to avoid severe desiccation and to absorb precious water before it percolates out of reach of its roots. It must become a supreme environmental opportunist or it will not survive.

The Genius of Beach Grass

Beach Grass (*Ammophila breviligulata*) has a genius for growing in sand. It has developed specific anatomical adaptations that make it one of the few plants to thrive in such an unstable environment as shifting sand.

Beach grass grows abundantly on barrier beaches from New England to the Virginia coast. South of Virginia a taller grass, Sea Oates (*Uniola paniculata*), takes over the task of pioneering dunes. Sea Oates is taller than the more northern beach grass, and has a fuller

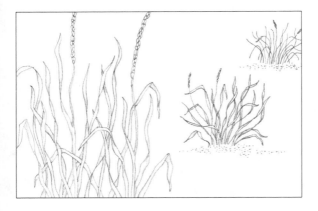

Figure 15 Beach grass has the unique ability to colonize bare sand areas by sending up new growth along its underground rhizomes.

seed head. Otherwise, its growing patterns are similar to beach grass. Beach grass will attempt to colonize any stretch of bare sand except on the beachfront itself, where the salt spray restricts its growth. Even there, clusters of beach grass are occasionally found, barely hanging on against the salt spray and the surf.

Beach grass is stimulated by moving sand. If it isn't being buried by sand it stops growing. New shoots trap sand particles which collect around the stem, forming a small mound. This stimulates the grass to put forth underground rhizomes that run under the sand's surface. Every few inches a shoot grows from special growth nodes scattered along the rhizomes. These underground rhizomes form a dense latticework that eventually binds an area of sand that may become a dune. In a mature stand of beach grass there is much more of the plant under the sand than grows above the surface.

Once the beach grass becomes established and the sand's movement stabilized, the beach grass stops growing. It reaches a maximum growth density and is no longer stimulated to send out new shoots. The mat of underground rhizomes and the plant's dense growth above ground stabilize the dune, and produce a protecting micro-climate on the sand's surface, providing the opportunity for other pioneer species to grow on the dunes.

Although this scenario sounds simple enough, beach grass must overcome some harsh conditions for it to thrive. To entrap rain before it percolates through the sand, it has developed two root systems. It sends down a series of long taproots that may reach forty feet in length. It also gains moisture from its rhizomes which run under the surface of the sand. The surface area of its roots is enormous; they are an effective adaptation to an environment that is as moisture-impoverished as a desert.

Figure 16 The underground rhizomes of beach grass are
        responsible for its ability to bind large areas of
        sand. Sometimes these rhizomes are uncovered
        when dunes are eroded during storms.

Once the beach grass collects the moisture, the
next task is to keep it. Its leaves and stems are
long and narrow, exposing a minimum of surface area to the drying heat, while performing
the necessary tasks of gas exchange and food
production from photosynthesis. On especially
hot, dry days, it rolls its leaves up in a tube,
producing a moist, "hot house" effect. This
action also conserves moisture by further reducing the surface area of the leaf.

It is easy to see the various stages by which
beach grass colonizes an area by looking at a
section of the dunes that has been recently
disturbed by storm-surges. "Wash-outs" are
places where new sand has been deposited by
the ocean breaching the primary dunes during
severe storms. Old dunes are torn down or split
in half, and the denuded dunes quickly spread
and bury adjacent areas. Here you can see
evidence of the process of beach grass colonization—a lush green carpet down the windward
side of an old dune, falling off to more scattered
colonies at the periphery of the new sand—
slowly marching across the new raw sand,
healing wounds in old dunes and creating new
dunes.

Beach grass grows best when it is being buried by sand at the rate of about four inches a year—too little sand movement and the grass grows slowly, too much and the grass is totally buried. But even if the grass is buried, it continues to send out rhizomes. These search out thinner depths of sand and form new stands of beach grass, sometimes several yards away from the parent plants.

It is common for a northeasterly storm to bury completely entire tracts of beach grass. If it isn't buried too deeply, it responds by sending up shoots to the surface to continue the colony. Successive storms may alternately bury and uncover the same tract of beach grass, forming a dense stratification of old plants, sometimes several feet thick. When erosion opens up the seaward side of primary dunes, it is common to see the whole top half of the dune comprised of layer upon layer of old-growth beach grass. Since the organic content of sand is almost sterile, the buried grass doesn't rot, as it would in a forest ecosystem with a more organic soil content. Instead it just piles up, forming a

Figure 17 Beach grass is responsible for building up the dunes. Without the ability of this remarkable grass to grow in sand, this overwash would probably not have healed into a new line of primary dunes.

Figure 18 Some dunes are so wind blown that large areas are perpetually open sand. This affect can also be produced by too much foot traffic on the dunes, which crushes the roots of the beach grass and kills the plant.

dense mat of grass and sand. This mat holds the sand with great tenacity; it is common to see a small dune that is severely eroded at its base, leaving a top-knot of matted grass and sand cantilevered into space.

Beach grass not only stabilizes sand and heals the ravages of storms and erosion, it also establishes windbreaks and protection from salt spray, giving the opportunity for other plant species to colonize the inter-dune area. Pure sand contains few nutrients that are usable by most plants. Sand is nitrogen poor, but plants such as beach pea, beach heather and bayberry are nitrogen fixers; they put nitrogen into the soil as part of their natural growing process. But beach pea or bayberry can't grow in moving sand and must depend on beach grass to first stabilize the sand so they can establish themselves.

Beach grass is the first step in establishing a soil rich enough in nutrients to support other, higher plant species. Its genius for growing in adverse conditions not only is responsible for the size and shape of many dunes, but also sets the stage for colonization by other plant species. This results in the development of the scrub thickets and forests that commonly grow throughout barrier islands. Without beach grass, and nothing to bind the sand, most of the vegetation common to barrier beaches would never have had a chance to become established. Barrier beaches would simply be sand spits, white scars of sand overrun by storms and shifting into the sea.

Other Plants That Bind the Sand and Build the Soil

Beach grass performs a unique role in that it is one of the few plants capable of colonizing in bare, moving sand. Once established, it creates enough of a stable surface micro-environment to allow other, less hardy plants to follow. These plants perpetuate the dune-building process, and some also actively improve the nutrients of the sand to make a soil. All these plants have two characteristics in common that make them excellent sand binders. Either they grow in dense colonies that impede the sand's movement, or their root systems are so extensive that they bind the sand under the surface. Some plants have both of these characteristics, and so make excellent sand binders and dune builders.

Beach Pea *(Lathyrus maritimus)* grows best in colonies. Dense, almost pure stands of beach pea may be found throughout the primary and interdune areas. It can propagate by seeds or by rhizomes that grow under the sand. Beach pea rhizomes are pale, fleshy, rather weak, and contain few root hairs. In dense stands the intermeshing rootlets can act as sand binders, but the real attribute of beach pea as a sand binder are the runners and tendrils that lie

Figure 19 Beach pea is a valuable nitrogen fixer.

along the surface, trapping moving sand. Beach pea is also a valuable nitrogen fixer, turning the sterile sand into the beginnings of a viable soil that will sustain more complex plant communities. Beach pea appears to resist salt spray damage more than some other dune plants, for I have seen it growing in dense, healthy stands on the backs of primary dunes right off the beach.

Beach pea likes to twine around beach grass for support. Many plots of beach grass on the primary dunes contain scattered growths of beach pea.

Mourning Doves and some song birds eat the tiny seeds, which look just like garden peas, but much smaller. I have broken open the tiny pods and snacked on the diminutive seeds, and found that they have the same fresh planty taste of garden peas. But it would take many hundreds of these peas, and hours of picking, to produce enough for just one meal.

Beach Heather *(Hudsonia tomentosa)* is a low, spreading, coarse plant, with scale-like leaves. From close up, beach heather looks like a miniature cedar forest. Its scaly leaves are covered with fine downy hairs which dampen the wind-blasted sands and reflect the hot sun. *Hudsonia* grows most abundantly along the New England coast, but it ranges south to North Carolina, where it appears infrequently.

Beach heather is an excellent sand binder, putting out a maze of small but very tough rootlets that form a network of fibers under the sand. Its sand-binding ability is further enhanced by the way it grows above the sand. It forms thick spreading mats that cover the sand's surface like a blanket. During dry weather, its leaves turn brown and brittle, starting from the bottom of the plant and moving up. Dead or old heather gets buried in the sand, acting as a platform that promotes new growth, eventually building up the dunes.

Although it can't stand direct exposure to salt spray, as can beach grass and sea rocket, beach heather does thrive between the dunes, or in any low area protected from high winds and salt spray. Sometimes it forms a wooly carpet of an acre or more.

Beach heather is vulnerable to trampling, especially during the dry late summer and fall months when its leaves become brittle. It grows slowly, and wounds created by careless walkers become long white scars that heal slowly and invite erosion.

Poison Ivy *(Rhus radicans)* is easily the most widespread plant on barrier islands. It deserves respect not only because of its virulent sap, but also because of its genius for adapting to almost any environmental situation.

Poison ivy grows from the primary dunes, where it is exposed to the rigors of the dune environment, to the fringes of the salt marsh that often forms the western border to many barrier islands. Poison ivy has evolved the ability to change the way it grows to meet these various environmental situations.

Poison ivy is an extremely adaptable plant and it can grow as a shrub, a vine, or as a ground

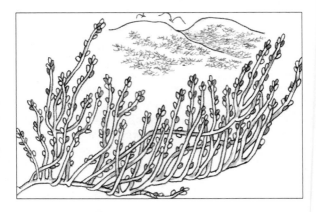

Figure 20 Beach heather's dense, tough roots make it an excellent sand binder, but its fragility makes it easily crushed by foot traffic.

Figure 21 Despite its bad reputation, poison ivy is an excellent sand binder and a valuable source of food and cover for birds and animals.

cover. In the dunes it takes the form of a low shrub. It creates a vast root system with many fine, but tough, root hairs sprouting along the length of the stems. A parent plant will send out many runners under the sand, and these runners will curve up and become new plants. A thick stand of poison ivy is an excellent sand binder; it is common to see stands of poison ivy growing atop a small dune, the sides of the dune having weathered away, leaving a topknot of poison ivy with its roots exposed. These decaying dunes illustrate poison ivy's ability to bind sand.

Poison ivy can propagate either by its runners or by its seed-carrying berries. These white berries are a favorite food of many birds that inhabit barrier beaches. A dense stand of poison ivy also makes excellent wildlife cover.

It is common to see swales (low-lying areas harboring thick stands of vegetation) throughout the dune area surrounded by a moat of poison ivy, giving way to the denser stands of other plants in the interior of the swale. This fringe of poison ivy has a secret blessing; it prevents human intruders from trampling the swales, leaving them pristine little islands of wildness.

Seaside Goldenrod *(Solidago sempervirens)* is the most spectacular of the seaside plants. Its tall, bushy stems, covered with long lance-like leaves, culminate in a brilliant yellow flower display in late summer. This plant grows from an underground root clump, with half a dozen or more stems growing to six-feet tall from one clump.

Seaside goldenrod is very salt resistant, often growing in scattered colonies along the upper beach and taking the full brunt of wind blast and salt spray. However, it prefers the backside of primary dunes and newly exposed sand areas such as the edges of moving sand dunes. It produces exceptionally tough roots: seaside goldenrod is capable of capping and holding a small dune all by itself. After a blowout, or in rapidly building sand areas, it is common to see several small dunes formed by pioneering goldenrod plants. These dunes may then merge and form a single dune or even a dune ridge with the help of other dune vegetation.

Often you will see goldenrod growing with dusty miller, their roots thickly entwined beneath the sand. This clot of roots makes a very efficient sand binder. Long after old dunes

Figure 22 From summer to early fall, the pretty yellow flowers of seaside goldenrod can be seen among the dunes.

Figure 23 Dusty miller has a wooly coat and small leaves, adaptations to an environment where retaining water is vital to its survival. These characteristics give it an advantage over other plants that try to grow in the dunes.

have blown away you will see a hump of sand held by the old root structures of these plants.

Dusty Miller *(Artemisia stelleriana)* was initially an introduced ornamental and was grown as a ground cover for gardens and lawns. It grows well in poor soil and has an interesting adaptation to prevent moisture loss. It is covered with a dense, wooly covering of fine, white hairs. Scientists believe that these hairs protect the plant from moisture loss, and the silvery color may reflect sunlight away from the plant. On a hot July afternoon, when the dunes become a bake oven, scrape some of the wooly covering off a leaf with your fingernail. You will uncover the succulent green surface of the leaf, and realize what an efficient insulator this fuzzy covering really is.

The roots of dusty miller are tough and extensive. One plant is capable of holding its own little dune, and it is common to see seaside goldenrod and dusty miller growing together—important partners in the dune-making process.

During July and August dusty miller has showy yellow flowers that grace the dunes. It grows from underground rhizomes, like beach grass, and so it is common to see a large parent plant, surrounded by generations of smaller plants, tenaciously holding onto their own small dune.

Bayberry (*Myrica pensylvanica*) is commonly found on barrier beaches from New England to the Outer Banks, but it is more abundant in its northern range. South of Fire Island it begins to mingle with, and is eventually replaced by, another very similar shrub, **Wax Myrtle** (*Myrica cerifera*). Both bayberry and wax myrtle occupy various habitats on barrier beaches: on the border between the salt marsh and the maritime forests, in coastal swamps or pocosins, in thickets between the dunes, and around the margins of swales hidden behind a dune ridge.

Where the range of wax myrtle and bayberry overlap they hybridize freely, and consistent identification can be difficult. Wax myrtle is the taller shrub, with smaller leaves and fruit, and bayberry is deciduous whereas wax myrtle is evergreen. Other than these differences, they grow in similar environments and contribute in similar ways to barrier beach ecosystems.

These shrubs are dominant in the thicket zones along the more protected western edge of barrier beaches. Here they grow alongside beach plum, black cherry and poison ivy, in stands so thick you can't push your way through them. Both bayberry and wax myrtle grow well on the protected sides of dunes that have already been colonized by other dune vegetation, such as beach grass, sea oates or seaside goldenrod. A clump of bayberry bushes can bind a large area of sand with its tough and extensive root system. Like beach pea, the roots of bayberry and wax myrtle produce nitrogen, which greatly enriches the soil. Their small, wax-coated fruits are eaten by many birds, most

Figure 24 Bayberry is an important member of the
thicket community. It grows in dense, almost
impenetrable hedges, providing excellent cover
for many kinds of wildlife.

notably by the various species of swallows that
mass on barrier beaches in late summer prior
to migration. These fruits contain a high percentage of fat, which the swallows use to fuel
their long southern migrations.

The bayberry was used by the colonists to
make scented candles. I have tried to duplicate
this feat, only to discover that it takes vast
quantities of laboriously picked berries and
much toil in smashing and cooking them in
large caldrons just to obtain a small amount
of wax!

Beach Plum *(Prunus maritima)* grows in thickets in much the same habitat as bayberry or
wax myrtle. Along with bayberry and poison
ivy, beach plum is one of the major constituents
of the dense thickets found in many protected
areas of barrier beaches. Its range is from
Maine to New Jersey, becoming less important
as a member of the thicket community south of
Fire Island.

The Indians relished the succulent plum, and
beach plum jelly was a staple of the colonists.
Many people still pick the plums in September,
and continue the old art of making the deli-

Figure 25 The beach plum is relished by the fox and is an important source of food for migrating birds in the autumn.

cious jelly. Along with the serviceberry fruit and the blueberry, both of which ripen in early summer, the beach plum is one of my favorite late summer nibbles. But pick only the dark blue or purple ones, and pick only plums that give a little when you pinch them between thumb and finger. The hard red plums are not yet ripe and will taste quite tart.

In May the beach plum puts on a gorgeous show of brilliant white flowers that dazzle the countryside. It is one of the earliest shrubs to bloom and its cottony-white blossoms are a sure sign that spring has finally arrived along the coast.

From Dunes to Forests

Beyond the beach and the salt spray, in areas protected by the leeward side of big-backed dunes, grow larger, more complex plant communities. These vary in size from scrub bushes occupying a few square feet to a mature forest of many acres. But where plants that pioneer dune areas are specialists in surviving in an adverse environment—a combination of the worst of desert and arctic conditions—the vegetation that grows in the interior of a mature barrier beach needs protection from salt spray and a permanent water source to guarantee success.

The dunes provide the salt spray protection. Even a small dune may deflect the salt spray just enough to enable a bayberry bush or a beach plum bush to grow. But a source of fresh water is necessary to support the stands of black gum, willow, red maple, aspen, gray birch, live oak and cherry trees that are found in profusion in the back areas of many barrier beaches. Indeed, many well-protected areas behind the dunes become fresh water swamps, with water-loving rushes, cattails and a whole

Figure 26 Dunes provide protection from salt spray. This shrub has been pruned into a ramp shape by the wind. Salt spray has been carried by turbulence over the brow of the dune and has killed back the top of the shrub to this unusual shape.

freshwater biota living only a few-score yards away from the salty ocean.

The source of this fresh water, which lies only a few feet beneath the sand's surface, is the unique bedrock and clay structures that under-lie many barrier beaches. These are saturated with ocean water that leaches down from the sea beach to form underground reservoirs. Barrier beaches are literally floating on a large underground layer of salt water, beneath which are saturated clays and gravel, all held up by interior water pressure.

Precipitation in the form of rain, snow and fog falls on the coast, percolates through the sand, and forms a lens of fresh water that floats on top of the large salt water deposit. This freshwater lens is from 1 to 50 feet deep, the depth depending on how large a space is left between the saturated clays and the sand. Where the bedrock undulates it pushes up the clay deposits—and hence the water table— sometimes very close to the sand's surface. This is the source of the ground water for the freshwater swamps that frequently occur on barrier beaches.

Houses on many developed barrier beaches depend on individual well points thrust into the sand that sip from the freshwater lens. On some barrier beaches, so much fresh water is being pumped that many houses draw salt-polluted water. On many overly developed bar-rier beaches this condition is already present; many residents must obtain their fresh water elsewhere.

Swales

Swales are depressions in the sand, ranging in size from a few feet across to several acres. Many swales contain a rich assortment of vegetation and are valuable nesting and feeding areas for much of the wildlife on a barrier beach.

Swales form when winds scour out a depression in the sand. This condition can happen in several ways: as a result of a washout created by a storm surge; from a dune that is destroyed during a storm, opening up a previously closed area to wind scour; or by the vortexes created as strong winds are channeled around the complex dune forms. Either way, once the wind has free purchase to a bare, relatively flat area of sand, it will eventually dig out a trough that usually becomes deeper with time.

The sand that the wind digs out is deposited as a small ridge at the head of the trough, which eventually may mature into a larger dune. Depending upon the trough's location, it may or may not develop into a swale. If the dune ridge at its head is built up enough, and if a ridge is formed at its foot by new sand from other dunes to its seaward side, *and* if its sides are flanked by high dunes, then it eventually may be protected enough to develop into a swale. However, it also may lack any one of these contingencies and end up being just a broad scar of sand, acting as a channel for sand transport into the interior of the dunes, until

Figure 27 Swales are pocket freshwater marshes in various stages of development. Some swales develop into fresh water ponds, like this pond hidden between the dune ridges at Nags Head Woods, Cape Hatteras.

another series of storms shifts the wind patterns around it and it gets filled in or buried by a moving dune.

Eventually, if the right conditions persist, the trough is dug deep enough by the wind that it comes within a few feet of the water table that underlies most barrier beaches. The trough may become a diminutive pond that holds water all year except for the driest summer months. The same wind action that originally digs out the trough begins to deposit sand into the water, and the pond slowly fills up with sediment. Water-loving black rush, cranberries, bunch grass and sometimes cattails grow in this miniature freshwater marsh area. The cranberries may spread to become a dense mat which covers most of the surface of the moist bottom of the trough. Willows may form isolated colonies on the fringes of the pond. The trough has become a swale. What was once a dry, desert-like area used only for sand transport into the interior of the dunes, now is a tiny protected refuge for special plants that can grow only in a freshwater environment.

A large variety of birds void seeds and drop debris into the swales. This provides a large reservoir of seeds and also increases the organic nutrients in the soil. After several seasons bayberry bushes form an impenetrable wall around the swale and poison ivy waves its potent leaves around the perimeter. Organic debris created by falling leaves, fruits and berries "sweeten" the soil, making it less acidic. A greatly improved soil and the availability of unlimited fresh water just a few feet below the surface of the swale create an environment suitable for plants that would otherwise die if their seeds landed on bare sand.

From seeds dropped by migrating birds, cherry trees, twisted and stunted like bonzai, emerge from the center of the swale. These, along with larger black willows, red maple, serviceberry, aspens, birches and the occasional black gum, represent the climax of the plants that can grow in a swale. Overall, these various processes produce a swale that is a thickly vegetated, moist-bottomed pocket refuge where birds nest, frogs live out their life-cycle, mosquitos breed and many other animals seek cover, food and water.

The swale's existence is transient. Eventually one side may build up into a dune ridge that may slowly bury it, or a severe storm may eradicate it altogether. On Plum Island, Massachusetts, there are many fine examples of deep, steep-sided swales. I have explored their interior during severe snowstorms; while the snow was being driven by the howling winds in blinding sheets outside, within the steep walls of the swale the snow fell softly in gentle swirls. Here a mature forest of old black cherry, red maple and serviceberry grows undisturbed. But the eastern dune ridge is rolling inexorably over the old swale; you can climb the eastern ridge and stand among small shrubs that are actually the tops of thirty-foot trees that have been buried recently by the moving dune. From this vantage point, you can see the past and future of the swale in one glance, and realize that the whole expanse of this barrier beach is a dynamic process of flex and flow, of many

Figure 28 These shrubs are really the tops of 60 foot trees, growing out of a swale, that have been buried by a massive dune ridge.

years of building up the complex dune shapes that can be changed irrevocably in a few hours by the fury of a northeasterly storm. But the storm just rearranges things, nothing is really lost. The remains of one destroyed dune are used to build several others. In a century or more, the eastern dune ridge may entirely bury the swale.

The Shrub/Thicket Community

Walking across a barrier beach can be akin to an obstacle course. Starting at the beach, the going is tough when you reach the loose sand at the base of the primary dunes. Unless you find a footpath or boardwalk across the primary dunes to the interior, don't attempt to climb them; it's not only exhausting for the climber, but detrimental to the structure of the dunes. Just a few careless climbers on the slip face of a dune can cause serious erosion.

Once past the primary dunes the going's pretty easy until you reach the edge of the maritime forest. As beach and heather give way to tangled stands of shrubs, you will encounter dense growths of bayberry or wax myrtle, often fringed with a moat of poison ivy. This area of shrubs, called the Shrub/Thicket Community, becomes so thick you can't push through them. Unless you find a deer trail that leads into the interior, their secrets will remain enclosed behind thickset branch and thorn.

North of Fire Island the thickets consist of bayberry, beach plum, honeysuckle, stunted cherry trees, greenbriar, Virginia creeper, and the ubiq-

Figure 29 Extensive thickets, with only scattered patches of loblolly pines, are typical of the pattern of vegetation found in the interior of low-lying barrier beaches, like Ocracoke Island in the Outer Banks.

Figure 30 Thickets are often so dense you can't push your way through them.

uitous poison ivy. Thickets on barrier beaches of the middle Atlantic coast consist of wax myrtle, bayberry, yaupon, holly and cherry trees, and even more of greenbriar and poison ivy.

The soil is richer around the thickets, and various interesting species of fungus and lichens grow in these protected areas. Lichens are a unique combination of fungus and algae in a symbiotic relationship. British Soldier lichen *(Cladonia cristatella)* can easily be identified by its fruits, which look like someone dabbed red nail polish on the tips of their tiny branches. Other branching lichen, like reindeer licken, can grow to encompass large patches that crunch under your feet during dry weather. Lichens have no root system and no leaves, but rely entirely upon whatever nutrients fall upon them by the wind. This kind of life support system is not as haphazard as it seems, for the air on barrier beaches is filled with tiny droplets of salt spray and dust particles that contain many nitrites and nitrate salts that the lichen use for nourishment.

A fungus seems an unlikely candidate to grow in sandy soils, since we are used to seeing them in cool, wet conditions. But the earth star *(Geaster triplex)* is common in the peripheral areas around thickets. This close cousin of the puffball has triangular-shaped "arms" surrounding a round center. Its thick outer layer curls up and becomes hard as leather during dry spells, but after a rain it softens, uncurls itself, and releases spores which are puffed out through a tiny hole when a drop of rain impacts the raised center. The appearance of earth stars signifies an enriched soil, for, as a fungus, they find nourishment from bits of organic material in the sand, such as decaying logs or pieces of dead leaves.

Dead leaves drop onto the sand, birds perch on the shrubs, adding their excrement to the sandy soil, and root systems probe and expand under the surface, aerating the sand and producing bacteria that aids in the decomposition of organic elements. The shrub/thicket community is one of the main synthesizers of nitrogen, potassium, and phosphorus into the soil.

Having spent many summers hiking New England barrier beaches—baking between the scorching sun and the white reflective dunes—I half expected to find the dunes of the Outer Banks of North Carolina littered with cactus fields, looking something like the southwest desert. Although at times it's just as parched as a desert, and the expanse of sand and dunes is very desert-like, the only cactus I found was the Prickly Pear *(Opuntia compressa),* which often forms large, spreading mats around the periphery of the shrub/thicket zone. It occurs sporadically south of Fire Island, becoming more common on Assateague Island and the Outer Banks. In summer it produces large pale yellow blooms with red centers. In the fall the cactus produces reddish-purple fruits which can be made into a fine jam. The prickly pear has few actual spines, but it is covered with fine hairs that are very irritating to the skin if the plant is handled. It stores water in its fleshy leaves, which have the capability to expand and contract, depending upon the availability of moisture.

Figure 31 Other plants besides shrubs inhabit the thicket community. The prickly pear cactus grows in open areas around the thicket.

The shrub/thicket community is really a buffer zone between the dunes and the maritime forests. As an ecological "edge," it contains organisms from both the dune and forest worlds, as well as life forms representing its own unique ecology. More birds nest and feed in the shrub/thicket zone than any other single area of a barrier beach. The thick growth provides cover for voles, mice, rabbits, foxes, and even some larger animals such as deer and wild horses.

Plum Island, Massachusetts, contains many extensive thicket areas tucked behind a large dune ridge. I have noticed many deer trails that trace across the heather, and almost all the trails lead to these thickets. I followed one especially well-worn trail until it entered a dark entrance beneath some bayberry bushes. I crouched on hands and knees and crawled into the thicket, shouldering my way along the narrow-arched trail until I was several hundred feet inside. Peering ahead I saw a sun-dappled clearing and there, bedded down among the leaves, were several deer either sleeping or chewing their cud. The deer seemed to take no notice of me, and I settled myself down into the leaves to observe them. Thrushes and white-throated sparrows swept through the thicket,

noisily tossing aside leaf litter, hoping to uncover some unexpected tidbit like a juicy insect
larvae or a spider. A pale version of Fowler's
Toad *(Bufo woodhousei)*, common on barrier
beaches, hopped lethargically across the deer
trail. A Beautiful Tiger Beetle *(Cicindela for-
mosa)*, a ferocious predator of ground dwelling
insects, scurried across the leaf litter, over my
arm, and disappeared into the shadows. A cat
bird landed close by and began its curious mew-
ing alarm call. Another cat bird joined the
first, and it was soon joined by a blackbird and
a grackle, all broadcasting their alarm calls
throughout the thicket. The intruder had been
discovered by the local constabulary. The deer
took no notice of the hubbub, except one old,
wise doe, who kept staring intently in the direction of the birds. She reluctantly stood up,
stretched herself, and slowly walked toward
where I lay. She stopped every few steps to
nibble at some leaves, always keeping a close
eye on the area in which I lay. The birds
seemed to redouble their calls at the approach
of the doe, and I lay amid the bayberry leaves
hardly daring to breathe. She stopped about
five feet from me. Still not quite making out
what was lying there, she stretched her neck
toward me, trying to smell what it was that
had suddenly appeared in the middle of her
trail. For a moment I looked into her enormous
moist brown eyes and then she jumped back,
let out a loud snort, and raced through the
deer beds with her white tail held straight up.
The other deer leaped from their resting places
and ran after her, their tails bobbing away
beyond the thin branches of the thicket.

I was impressed by how quickly the deer disappeared, almost without a sound, into the farthest reaches of the thicket. Their mad
scramble lasted only a few seconds, and yet,
even as it was happening, the thick foliage
muted their panicked retreat into a sound like
wind roving the leaves. Somewhat embarrassed
as to the commotion I had caused, I backed out
of the trail and stood up to survey the expanse

of the thicket. The cat birds were calling more than ever, shaming me into walking back toward the beach and leaving their shrubby fortress to its own kind of solitude. I admired how appropriate a home the thickly entwined shrubs were for so many of the wild creatures on barrier beaches.

Maritime Forests

When John Smith explored the Cape Ann area of Massachusetts in 1614, he wrote the first European description of Plum Island, a barrier beach located by the mouth of the Merrimack River:

> On the east is an Isle of two or three leagues in length; the one half plain marsh grass fit for pasture, with many fair high groves of Mulberry trees and gardens; and there is also oaks, pines, and other woods to make this place an excellent habitation, being a good and safe harbor.

From early descriptions and modern biological studies, it is evident that Plum Island was heavily wooded in places, with a good stand of pine and oak. These were probably representations of climax forests, with small freshwater swamps and bogs scattered throughout the low-lying areas.

The early history of many barrier beaches has similar references to stands of pines or oak forests extending down their western edge. Some low, narrow barrier beaches, like some areas of the Outer Banks of North Carolina, were probably never very heavily vegetated. With no salt spray protection, and constant inlet formation and washouts burying large tracks of the interior with sand, any substantial vegetation cover would get blown out before it could ever get started. But where the barrier beach is wider and is more stable, with a wider, higher, interdune area, forests often develop that rival in diversity and extent those found on the mainland. Although most maritime forests were cut down shortly after they were colonized, some excellent examples of these forests have been preserved. Buxton Woods and Nags Head Woods, on Cape Hatteras, North Carolina, and the Sunken Forest on Fire Island, New York, are examples of maritime forests that have been preserved, either through the National Park Service, the Federal Wildlife Refuge system, or through private interests.

The maritime forests, from New England to New Jersey, are dominated by the **Pitch Pine** *(Pinus rigida)*. Pitch pine can grow as tall as fifty feet in mainland forests, but along the coast it rarely grows over thirty feet tall. Salt spray gives the pitch pine a windswept, contorted shape. One of the most dramatic sights on a barrier beach is a pitch pine, knarled and twisted like bonzai, growing from an eroded dune. A pitch pine forest usually has an impenetrable thicket surrounding it, often made up of bayberry, poison ivy and greenbriar, making access to the forest seemingly impossible. It is usually necessary to find a boardwalk or a deer trail that breaks through the thicket into the interior in order to investigate the maritime forest. Once inside, it is remarkably easy to walk through because the dead pine needles on the forest floor mulch the understory clear of entangling brush.

Pitch pines have needles which are slightly twisted and grouped in clusters of three. The length of the needles vary from two to four inches. The seed cone is ovid in shape and rather small in size. Pitch pine is also associated with red maple, grey birch, aspen, sassafrass, and some oaks.

Figure 32 Interior of maritime forest comprised of loblolly pine. Assateague Island, Virginia.

Figure 33 Interior of maritime forest comprised of many hardwood species. This diverse, broad-leaved forest, containing many species of oaks, beeches, maples, and pines, might take many hundreds of years to achieve this level of maturity. This type of forest development may represent a final climax stage beyond the loblolly pine forest. Nags Head Woods, Cape Hatteras, North Carolina.

Pitch pine was used by the colonists as fire wood, for the tree contains a high percentage of flammable resins. These resins were the source for pitch, which was processed into tar and used for caulking wooden ships. In the more undisturbed portions of the forests, the pitch pine is often used as heronries and rookeries, and the crow and owl are common nesters.

The **Loblolly Pine** *(Pinus taeda)* takes over as the principle tree of the maritime forest from New Jersey south to Florida. It has much longer needles than the pitch pine—five to ten inches in length—and they come in bundles of three. The seed cone is elongated and is three to six inches long. Loblolly pines grow as tall as 90 feet in the extensive pine forests of the piedmont and coastal plain areas of the mid-Atlantic, rarely growing taller than 50 feet in the maritime forests.

Barrier beaches are in the process of healing after hundreds of years of abuse. The thick stands of pine that make up the maritime for-

ests on some of our barrier beaches today, are
merely shadows of the extensive forests that
grew behind the dunes before the coast was
colonized. Many of the forests on the Outer
Banks and Cape Cod have been planted by
conservation programs in the last fifty years.
Nags Head Woods, on Cape Hatteras, represents the last great tract of climax maritime
forest to be seen on any barrier beach. This
maritime forest has been essentially untouched
for over 1500 years, and the result is a diversity
of species and a luxurious growth that rivals
any forest on the mainland. Indeed, because of
its unique location, Nags Head Woods contains
many rare species found either much further
south or north of Cape Hatteras.

Walking the cool shady lanes of Nags Head
Woods is like going back in time. The forest is
situated among a complex of dunes that reach
heights of over 100 feet. There are beech trees
that have lived long enough to have witnessed
the soft footfalls of the Indians as they hunted
deer and turkey in the forest. Moss-draped live

Figure 34 Dunes not only create the protection needed for
the maritime forests to grow, but a dune ridge
on the move can also destroy an entire forest.
This dune is about 110 feet in height and is
slowly burying a large tract of climax maritime
forest at Nags Head Woods.

oaks canopy a swale that is so old and extensive it resembles a Georgia swamp. Twice as many species of oaks grow from a single dune flank in this forest than in all the forests of New England.

Nags Head Woods may represent the pinnacle of ecological development of a maritime forest. If our barrier beaches had remained pristine, perhaps many more maritime forests would now share the unique flora and fauna of Nags Head Woods.

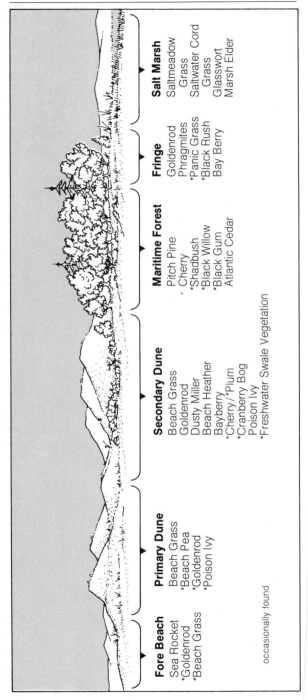

Salt Marsh
Saltmeadow Grass
Saltwater Cord Grass
Glasswort
Marsh Elder

Fringe
Goldenrod
Phragmites
*Panic Grass
*Black Rush
Bay Berry

Maritime Forest
Pitch Pine
· Cherry
*Shadbush
*Black Willow
*Black Gum
Atlantic Cedar

Secondary Dune
Beach Grass
Goldenrod
Dusty Miller
Beach Heather
Bayberry
*Cherry/*Plum
*Cranberry Bog
Poison Ivy
*Freshwater Swale Vegetation

Primary Dune
Beach Grass
*Beach Pea
*Goldenrod
*Poison Ivy

Fore Beach
Sea Rocket
*Goldenrod
*Beach Grass

*occasionally found

Figure 35 Cross-section of the major ecological zones of a typical barrier beach found in New England.

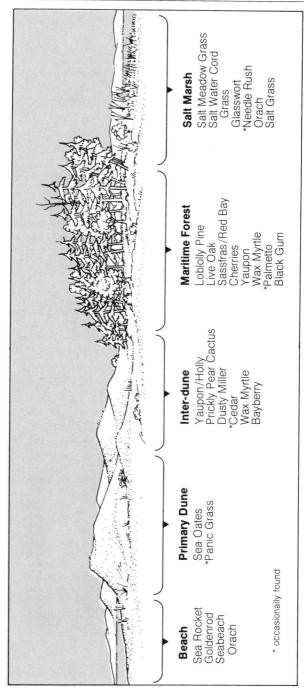

Salt Marsh
Salt Meadow Grass
Salt Water Cord
  Grass
Glasswort
*Needle Rush
Orach
Salt Grass

Maritime Forest
Loblolly Pine
Live Oak
Sassfras/Red Bay
Cherries
Yaupon
Wax Myrtle
*Palmetto
Black Gum

Inter-dune
Yaupon/Holly
Prickly Pear Cactus
Dusty Miller
*Cedar
Wax Myrtle
Bayberry

Primary Dune
Sea Oates
*Panic Grass

Beach
Sea Rocket
Goldenrod
Seabeach
  Orach

* occasionally found

Figure 36 Cross-section of the major ecological zones of a typical barrier beach of the mid-Atlantic coastline.

The Salt Marsh

Fifteen years ago, on one of my first trips to a salt marsh, I become stranded in my canoe at low tide in one of the tidal creeks that are etched onto the flat, green surface of the marsh. Having nothing to do but wait until the tide came in again to float me free, I took off my shoes and socks and waded around the creek. I discovered a miniature world populated by strange and alien creatures, and my appetite was whetted to learn more about them. In the intervening years, I have spent hundreds of hours exploring the salt marsh and learning some of its secrets, although scientific investigation about the ecology of the salt marsh is just beginning to bear fruit.

To the early colonists, the salt marsh was generally considered to be a nuisance. Its fogs and strange odors were held responsible for sickness and death. Although early farmers gladly harvested the thick, abundant marsh grass, and used the taller species of marsh grass for thatching the roofs of their dwellings, their superstitions kept them from venturing onto the marsh at night for fear it would swallow them up or they would contract a mysterious disease and go mad. Although now it is known

Figure 37 The salt marsh is one of the most productive environments in the world.

that the salt marsh isn't responsible for any of these effects, it has always been considered nothing more than a troublesome barrier to economic development. But modern studies have shown that the salt marsh is an important breeding and developing grounds for many of the important foodfishes, gamefish and shellfish species that form a cornerstone of the economy of this region. As a fascinating ecosystem, it deserves to be preserved and studied with the same enthusiasm as is given other, better known ecosystems.

How a Salt Marsh is Formed

When a barrier beach is first formed, a protected cove usually develops on its western side that may include fresh water flushed into it from rivers. The cove becomes an estuary (an area where fresh and salt water mix), and a marsh is formed, comprised of cattails and various kinds of rushes that can grow in fresh and brackish water. With the gradually rising sea level, and the eventual silting-in of the freshwater marsh, a salt marsh is formed that eventually grows over the old freshwater marsh area. Core tests have shown that underlying the salt marsh that rings the western edge of many barrier beaches is a peat deposit formed by this early freshwater marsh. Using modern artifact dating techniques, scientists have determined that the present saltmarsh complex of our barrier beaches are from two to four thousand years old.

The Ecology of the Salt Marsh

A salt marsh is a nutrient pumping station; it takes in essential minerals and salts from the sea on each incoming tide and releases organic material into the estuarine system on the outgoing tide. This system is greatly dependent upon specialized plants that thrive in conditions that would kill most other land plants. While beach grass has many special characteristics that enable it to thrive in an otherwise hostile environment, making it the cornerstone of the sand dune community, specialized types of salt marsh grasses perform a similar role in the development and maintenance of the salt marsh. Two types of salt marsh grass are important to this process: Saltwater Cord Grass *(Spartina alterniflora)* and Saltmeadow Grass *(Spartina patens)*.

The Genius of Salt Marsh Grasses

The *Spartina* grasses are specialized to grow in a salt marsh environment, and are able to withstand inundation by salt water—a condition that would kill most other types of plants. The salt marsh is divided into two broad areas, the upper, or drier part, and the lower, or wetter section. The lower section is usually covered by tidal water twice a day, and the taller **Saltwater Cord Grass** *(Spartina alternaflora),* grows best here. It pioneers new mudflats and the lower areas of the salt marsh that are commonly covered by high tides. It reproduces by flowering and spreading its seeds by the wind, like most other grasses, but if its seeds drop on hostile ground (for they are relished by many birds), the plant can still continue its propagation by sending out underground rhizomes. These rhizomes form a thick mat of interlaced roots that binds the soft mud into a platform which gives the plant enough of a purchase to continue to colonize new areas—thereby building up the marsh, sometimes as much as six inches a year. Saltwater Cord Grass can be identified easily in a salt marsh, for it is usually taller than the saltmeadow grass and grows around the wetter sections of the lower salt marsh and along the sides of the tidal creeks. Look along a tidal creek in the salt marsh and the taller grass that grows around the raised edges of the creek will almost certainly be Saltwater Cord Grass.

Saltmeadow Grass *(Spartina patens)* is the dominant grass in the higher marsh, and is only covered by saltwater in high spring tides, which may occur once or twice a month. This is a much shorter, thinner-stemmed grass, which from a distance resembles a well-manicured fareway on a golf course. Unlike saltwater cord grass, it doesn't grow straight, but lies down in thick mats on the marsh surface. A closer examination reveals that each stem is made of segments jointed together at a slight angle. These joints flex easily, and when high spring tides flood the high marsh, the swirling water often creates curious circular depressions, which look like matted beds made by deer in the grass. Flexible joints help the plant withstand occasional structural stresses caused by the swirling tidal waters, for the joints will bend before the plant breaks. These mats also create a greenhouse effect; underneath the thick mat the soil stays relatively moist, even during the most severe drought. On a hot day, lift up a handful of the saltmeadow grass and you will see many creatures, mostly insects, going about their business, hardly aware of the heat on the surface.

The Food Chain of the Salt Marsh

Because the lower marsh is washed by the tides twice a day, it receives a steady supply of nutrients supplied by the sea. One problem for creatures that must live in the lower marsh is that the salinity of the water can radically change in a short period of time. A sudden rainstorm can alter the salinity of a marsh pool from salty to almost fresh, while the same pool can contain abnormal concentrations of salt if left a few days to evaporate in the hot summer sun. The salinity of even the larger tidal creeks can change dramatically, depending on whether the tide is coming in or going out, and the creek's proximity to the estuary. For an organism to survive in the salt marsh, it must be capable of adapting to extreme fluctuations in salinity. It must also be capable of surviving either out of water or underwater, for limited periods of time, depending upon the level of the tides.

Several kinds of algae grow in abundance in the salt marsh. Green and brown algae flourish throughout the marsh and on the mudflats. It forms dense mats as much as a half-inch thick on the mud at the base of the saltwater cord grass and on the bottom of the saltwater pools scattered throughout the marsh. Algae forms the most abundant food item at the bottom of the food chain in the salt marsh, and many other salt marsh creatures depend upon algae as a basic food source. Twice a day the tides wash out bits of algae, along with numerous other kinds of debris, into the estuary, where much of it becomes stranded on the mudflats during low tide. Exposed to the air, it is immediately attacked by bacteria and fungi, which begins the process of reducing the debris to its basic elements.

Suspension feeders, such as clams, mussels, and several types of marine worms, feed on this rich soup by passing large amounts of water through their systems and filtering out the bacteria, algae, and other nutrients. The Ribbed Mussel *(Modiolus demissus)* is very common on the low marsh, where it can be found in large colonies jammed into the mud at the base of the cord grass. It not only feeds by filtering out organic material, but greatly adds to the organic content of the water by excreting the inedible material, bound by mucus, as "pseudofeces." These excretions attract enormous amounts of bacteria and fungi, which are then washed into the system at the next high tide. Many other small organisms burrow amid the mussels to dine on these excretions. Most suspension feeders replace nutrients into the salt marsh system by producing waste materials that are food for bacteria, fungi, and other salt marsh invertebrates. They are responsible for reworking essential nutrients for other animals along the food chain.

The edible Blue Mussel *(Mytilus edulis)* is also one of the most numerous filter feeders of the mudflats in the open waters of the estuary. They attach themselves firmly to the mud by long sessile fibers. Dead mussels are used as

Figure 38 The ribbed mussel grows in dense colonies at the base of the saltwater cord grass.

anchors for other mussels, and many layers are sometimes built up on the mudflats. This hard surface of many layers of mussels attracts organisms that would normally be found among a rocky coast, or along the coast of Maine. Periwinkles, barnacles, crabs, and sometimes starfish and lobster frequent these mussel beds. Mussel beds flourish in estuaries where tidal currents keep them bathed in oxygen-rich water and bring them an abundant supply of food. You may find extensive blue mussel beds by the mouths of rivers where they pour into the estuary behind the barrier beach.

Deposit feeders graze on the diatoms, dinoflagellates, feces, algae and other debris on the surface of the mud. Snails are a common type of deposit feeder, and several kinds are very common on the mudflats and in the salt marsh. One of the most interesting snails is the Salt Marsh Snail *(Melampus bidentatus)*, which can be found in enormous numbers at the base of the saltwater cord grass in the lower marsh. This snail has the interesting characteristic of having a tiny lung with which it breathes. It escapes the rising tide by climbing up the stems of the cord grass to graze on the algae and other microorganisms covering the stems and leaves. When the tide recedes, it travels down the stems to the mud below, which pro-

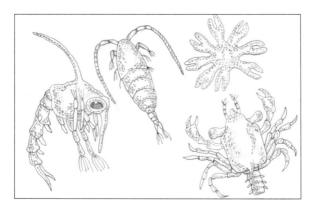

Figure 39 Along with algae, zooplankton are an important part of the food chain in the salt marsh creeks. These bizarrely-shaped animals are copepods and the larvae of various kinds of crabs and shellfish.

tects it from desiccation and predation. Other snails in the tidal creeks of the salt marsh are the Mud Dog Whelk *(Nassarius obsoletus),* and other closely related snails of the genus *Nassa.* These snails are the most numerous medium-sized snails on the mudflats. They are predatious on other snails, and they don't mind if their most recent victim is another whelk.

Salt marsh pans are the home of the tiny snail *Hydrobia minuta,* which is only about one-seventh of an inch long. This minute snail is sometimes so numerous that I have counted as many as one hundred to the square inch! From a distance they look like tiny pieces of black gravel scattered on the mud, but a closer scrutiny reveals their erratic movement. Like miniature bumper cars, they cruise the mud's surface for diatoms, algae, and bits of debris. Their range is from Maine to New Jersey.

The enormous population of algae, bacteria, fungi, snails, and other small organisms that exist in relation to them, sets up a very broad-based food source for higher organisms in the salt marsh. Predatory polychaete worms, like the common Blood Worm *(Glycera dibranchiata)* (the worm most often used as bait by surf fishermen) burrows beneath the mud, preying on small nematode worms, and smaller clam worms. They have four sharp fangs with which they can bite prey, and human fingers, alike. The Green Crab *(Carcinus maenas)* is the most abundant crab in the mudflats and the salt marsh, and it preys upon almost anything that it can grab with its small pincers. It especially relishes small clams and mussels, and can wipe out an entire clam bed if the crab becomes too numerous. Fortunately, the herring gull, black-backed gull, various herons and even some larger fish place the green crab high on their menus.

Predation in the salt marsh and on the mudflats is attuned to the cycle of the tides. Large fish, like the flounder, and other kinds of predators, like the horseshoe crab and the delicious blue crab, move into the salt marsh creeks at high tide. Here they prey on a wide variety of burrowing worms and small clams. At low tide, when large areas of the mudflats and most of the salt marsh creeks are exposed, the snails roam on the surface of the mud, grazing on the debris left from the previous tide. However, birds take advantage of the hordes of feeding snails, and many kinds of herons, egrets, yellow legs, and other types of shore birds fill their bellies with the snails,

Figure 40 Snails litter the mudflats of the salt marsh.

Figure 41 When low tide exposes the mudflats, snails graze on the sheen of algae growing on the surface of the mud.

burrowing worms, amphipods, prawns, and innumerable other creatures forming the base of the food chain in the salt marsh. These nutrients move up the food chain; the green crab which picks the clam worm out of its burrow gets eaten by the patient great blue heron. All inhabitants of the salt marsh benefit from the enormous nutritive production of the estuary, mudflats and, finally, by the salt marsh itself.

Other benefits of the salt marsh are not so much ecological as aesthetic; rarely do we have the opportunity to gaze at such a vista as the salt marsh offers to the patient observer. Laid open to the elements, it acts as a sensitive photographic negative, letting the rest of nature imprint itself upon its surface. Many of the dynamic processes of the salt marsh are so complex that they remain a mystery. Their individual functions intertwine to such an extent with all other processes of the salt marsh that to study a single animal or plant in isolation seems futile. Leave aside, for the moment, the scientific reference books, the dip nets, the collecting bottles, the note books and the technical jargon. To become stranded at low tide on a mudflat, and experience the incredible diversity and fecundity of the salt marsh is just as good a way of learning about the salt marsh as any other.

Salt Marsh Pools

Higher sections of the salt marsh are dotted with stagnant pools, sometimes called *saltpans*, of various size, ranging from a foot in diameter to ponds of several acres. Their formation is a mystery. Some scientists believe they are formed from "rotten" spots on the salt marsh where the grass has died, or they may be cut-off sections of old, overgrown marsh creeks. Another interesting theory is that in the winter, heavy chunks of ice break off from the tidal creeks and float over the salt marsh during high tides, and these may scrape out raw spots in the marsh that become saltpans. Whatever the cause, saltpans represent the most extreme environment of the salt marsh.

Unusually high tides or heavy rains fill the saltpans throughout the marsh. But the summer winds and sun soon begin to evaporate the water, and the salinity of a typical saltpan can change from being almost fresh to extremely salty in a matter of days. Whatever organisms live in this hellish environment must be extremely tough and adaptable. Sheets of brown and green algae carpet the bottom, and bacteria thrive on the algae that is exposed to the air around the edge of the pool. Mosquito larvae can suddenly appear, especially after a heavy rain, and several days later the infamous salt marsh mosquito will hatch and swarm over the area. They make a walk in the salt marsh in summer an ordeal involving bug sprays, headnets and anti-itch lotions. Some water insects, notably the water boatman, usually an insect of the freshwater marsh, can live in great numbers in these salty pools. Even fish can thrive in the saltpans. The common Mummichog (*Fundulus heteroclitus*) and various species of Sticklebacks (*Gasterosteus* sp.) are small fish commonly found in saltpans and tidal creeks throughout the salt marsh. If these fish are stranded in the saltpans by a high spring tide, they will usually escape when the tidal waters fill the pools again.

The summer sun rapidly accelerates evaporation from the pools, and many dry up completely by August, leaving a dry, leather-like coating of desiccated algae—which is usually coated with encrusted salt crystals. The mud cracks and dries hard like tough leather and what little water remains is in the deepest pools, which are crowded with fish and insects making their last stand against annihilation. This concentrated food source draws large numbers of wading birds which gorge themselves until they can barely fly. Living in such an environment is a little like being suddenly transported from the relative security of a pond to Death Valley. But the algae will reconstitute itself in the next rain; the water boatman will survive by hiding deep in the cracks of the mud; mosquito eggs can lie dormant for weeks; and the stranded fish will simply bury themselves in the mud and wait for the next spring tide to float them to freedom.

Saltpans create a favorite area to see all types of wading birds, and many unusual migrant birds use salt pans as well. Smaller pools dot the salt marsh, each pool a concentrated food source for the many birds that use the marsh through the year.

Any discussion of the salt marsh would not be complete without a mention of two summer terrors, the Salt Marsh Mosquito (*Aedes sollicitans*) and the Greenhead Fly (*Tabinid sp.*). The salt marsh mosquito has a life cycle that is uniquely adapted to the environment of the salt marsh. Like all other types of mosquitos, the larvae need water to flourish, but unlike other species, the larvae of the salt marsh mosquito can tolerate high levels of salt.

Through millions of years of evolution, the mosquito has developed some clever tricks to guarantee that her offspring survive to pester you at your next cookout. The female mosquito deposits about one hundred eggs on the moist mud banks of salt marsh tidal creeks. To avoid the ravenous mosquito-eating fishes of the creeks, she usually chooses mud banks that only flood during spring tides. The eggs quickly develop hard shells, which protect them from desiccation. This hard shell allows the eggs to dry completely and to withstand the hot summer sun that can sometimes dry the mudflats to the consistency of pottery shards. When spring tides flood the eggs, they hatch within a few hours into larvae and begin to feed furiously on floating bits of algae and micro-organisms that inhabit the wet mud and saltpans. The larvae have a very short life cycle, and given ideal conditions, it may take only four days for the larvae to pass through to the adult form.

The first two days in the life of an adult salt marsh mosquito is reserved for mating, after which they migrate in great numbers to the grassy areas of the marsh. Both males and females suck plant juices for sustenance, but the female has a great drive to suck blood. A meal of blood makes the female many times more fertile than a diet of plant juices, so natural selection has produced a mosquito that is very aggressive in pursuit of its victim. Females will fly up to ten miles away from their hatching areas to find a meal.

The salt marsh mosquito has an array of built-in sophisticated sensing devices that make the most modern fighter aircraft technology seem obsolete by comparison. It can home in on any warm-blooded animal from many feet away by using its infra-red sensors. It can not only find you in total darkness, it can even tell what part of your body is exposed by finding those blood vessels that are close to the surface of the skin. It can also detect the presence of a warm-blooded creature by the carbon dioxide that all oxygen-breathing animals expel during respiration. Next time you walk in the salt marsh, if you can stop your swatting long enough to be observant, notice that many of the mosquitos seem to "home in" on your breath. Mosquitos often fly zig-zag patterns in front of your face, sensing your carbon dioxide.

Although their eyesight is poor compared to some other flying insects, they have enough sight acuity to detect movement and colors easily. They seem particularly attracted to dark colors; experiments have shown that they are most attracted to the color blue. Their usual mode of operation is to hang onto a blade of salt marsh grass until some movement stimulates them to further investigate the disturbance.

The female salt marsh mosquito is attracted to high body temperatures, so it really prefers small animals with high metabolic rates, like mice or birds, as opposed to larger, lower-temperature animals, like humans. However, given the odds against one out of a billion mosquitos finding *any* warm-blooded animal in the vastness of the salt marsh, no matter what its size or body temperature, it's no wonder that it only takes a few steps into the salt marsh to attract them in hordes.

Some advice for travelers on the salt marsh. Try to pick windy days with cooler temperatures and low humidity for your walks on the salt marsh. The mosquito can fly at a top speed of seven miles per hour. A steady breeze of ten miles per hour will keep most of them away.

Wear light-colored clothing. Pants and a long-sleeve shirt and a hat or scarf to cover your head will protect you more completely than shorts and a T-shirt. While hiking with companions in the salt marsh I noticed that whenever I wore light-colored clothing, I attracted very few mosquitos, while my friends, in blue jeans and dark shirts, were covered with the pests. A hat keeps them off your head and out of your hair.

Recent experiments have shown that mosquitos have a good sense of smell, and seem to be attracted to people who have recently eaten fruits—especially bananas. They also are attracted to perspiration and sweet-smelling deodorants. If all this is beginning to sound as if the mosquito has the upper hand in all of this, you're right, it does! Even if you had just showered, used no deodorant, wrapped yourself in a white sheet, held your breath, and went out in a hurricane, you'd still be met with a horde of hungry mosquitos when you walked into the salt marsh. It's just that this horde would be smaller than the horde that would assail you if you *didn't* take these precautions.

Even though the salt marsh mosquito has many unsavory characteristics, its contribution to the food chain of the salt marsh can't be overlooked. Mosquito eggs and larvae are a major food of many of the fish and insects that inhabit the tidal creeks and saltpans of the marsh. A whole legion of predators, from the dragon fly to the bank swallow, depend on the adult salt marsh mosquito for their livelihood. Although millions of dollars have been spent on mosquito control programs—everything from draining the salt marsh, to digging drainage ditches, to spraying with powerful insecticides—no program has proven itself successful in destroying the mosquito. Before the federal government passed the Wetlands Acts, hundreds of thousands of acres of salt marsh was destroyed for mosquito control and development. Recent ecological studies have revealed that most natural salt marshes produce far fewer mosquitos than those salt marshes that have been ditched to reduce the mosquito population. Extensive tidal creeks and saltpans breed large populations of mosquito-eating fish, which consume the larvae and control the adult mosquito population.

As with the salt marsh mosquito, only the female greenhead fly bites humans while the male feeds only on plant juices. She lays her eggs on the stems or leaves of the *Spartina* grasses, and when the larvae hatch out, they crawl down and burrow into the mud. Here they begin a life of predation, eating just about anything they can grasp with their sharp jaws. They change into adult flies by the latter part of summer, and by the last two weeks of July are at their peak. By the end of August they have almost entirely disappeared. The female's bite is painful because she rips a piece of skin off with her powerful mandibles and then sucks the blood.

Nature has given the greenhead fly some potent weapons to be used against us. It is actually a horsefly, capable of flying at speeds of more than fifty miles per hour, so nothing short of a hurricane will deter them. They have huge, bulging eyes that can spot movement at several yards. Like the mosquito, they seem to be color sensitive, having a preference for dark shades of blue or black. While not as numerous as the mosquito, they make up in ferocity what they lack in numbers. Except for wearing lots of light-hued clothes, there isn't much you can do to deter them at the height of their season. During the last week of July many sunbathers are driven off the beach by these terrors.

Greenheads rely upon their excellent eyesight during the day to find and pursue their victims, so at sunset they drop down to the grass to rest until the next morning. Remaining sensitive to the greenhead's role in nature is difficult when they're circling around your head waiting their chance to deliver a painful bite, but they *are* an important food source in the ecology of the salt marsh. The larvae is fed upon by many of the smaller predators of the mud flats, including crabs and shore birds. Many thousands of greenhead flies are crammed down the throats of young swallows, fly catchers and kingbirds every season, providing an important source of protein to these growing broods.

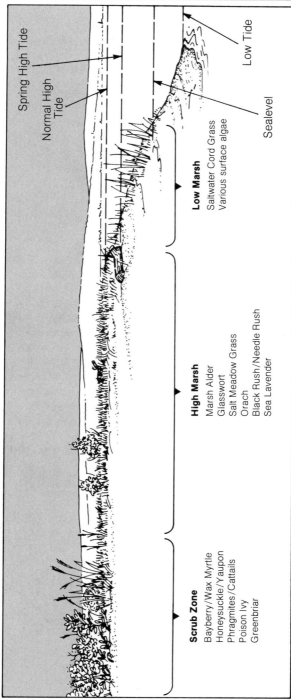

Spring High Tide

Normal High Tide

Low Tide

Sealevel

Low Marsh
Saltwater Cord Grass
Various surface algae

High Marsh
Marsh Alder
Glasswort
Salt Meadow Grass
Orach
Black Rush/Needle Rush
Sea Lavender

Scrub Zone
Bayberry/Wax Myrtle
Honeysuckle/Yaupon
Phragmites/Cattails
Poison Ivy
Greenbriar

Figure 42 Cross-section of the ecological zones of a typical
   salt marsh.

Predator and Prey Animals of the Barrier Beach

Animals must feed on other living things to survive; that's a hard and fast rule of nature. In general, the ecology of animals is divided into those animals that feed on plants, or prey species, and those animals that feed on the prey species, or the predators. There isn't always a neat division between predator and prey animals; these distinctions are meant to describe general characteristics apparent throughout the animal kingdom. This great movable feast, where everything is snacking on everything else, is called the *food chain*.

Animals of the Food Chain

It is generally true that the smaller animals are prey for a larger predator. A successful prey animal must reproduce rapidly and have a large repertoire of tricks to escape the many predators which hunt it. From the predators' point of view, a successful prey animal should be abundant, generally available to a variety of predators, and be incautious or clumsy enough to be caught at least some of the time.

Major Prey Animals of the Barrier Beach

Meadow Vole *(Microtus pennsylvanicus)* is probably the single most important prey animal on the barrier beach. It is also known as the meadow mouse, although it isn't really like most mice, and is a separate species with very mouse-like habits. The meadow vole differs from most mice in having smaller ears that are not prominent, and a much smaller tail that is furred, as opposed to the normally naked tail of mice. Its fur is like that of a mole, very soft and a dark chestnut brown, with a few coarse guard hairs.

Voles live in grass and make their nests out of balls of grass which contain other animal fur, feathers, bits of fluff—anything they can gather to make their nest soft and cozy. They don't

Figure 43 Meadow voles construct extensive tunnels under the grass to hide their activities from their many enemies. Sometimes sections of these tunnels become visible on the surface of the snow.

hibernate as do some mouse species. During the winter they construct extensive burrows underneath the grass and snow and continue their busy existence out of sight of their many predators. You can easily see these tunnels when the snow thaws. Some of these tunnels are used as thoroughfares and others are used for food storage and breeding chambers. Since the vole does not hibernate, but remains active throughout the year, it must store enormous quantities of grass (its favorite food), nuts and seeds in these tunnels. I have discovered tunnel cul-de-sacs stuffed with enough grass to make a wad the size of a soccerball! And most voles have several of these storage areas in their individual territories.

Voles are hunted by just about every animal predator that occur on barrier beaches—the fox, marsh hawk, weasel, rough-legged hawk, short-eared and great-horned owls, etc. It's a good thing they are hunted so intensively, because just one female vole is capable of breeding up to seventeen times in a year, becoming sexually mature at the ripe old age of three weeks! Since one mile of a typical barrier beach probably harbors several hundred voles, the world would be quickly overrun with them if their numbers were not greatly reduced by predators and disease. Without the lowly vole many of the predators on barrier beaches would starve.

Voles love grassy areas, so they can be found in greatest abundance in upland fields, overgrown drumlins, the thick cover provided by swales, or at the brushy edge of the barrier beach.

The **White-footed Mouse** *(Peromyscus leucopus)* is one of the most beautiful little creatures I have ever seen. It reminds me of a Disney character, for it is the quintessence of what a mouse should look like. White-footed mice have light brown backs, creamy white bellies, white-furred feet and long, naked tails. Their chief attributes are their large ears and enormous, liquid-black eyes. They share the same lowly position on nature's ecological ladder as the vole; they are a basic food item for many predators.

Their habits differ markedly from the vole, however, in that they prefer scrub and forests, rather than open meadows. They make their tidy fur-lined nests in almost any hole or crevice in the trees, and sometimes they refurbish

Figure 44 The nibbled caps of mushrooms are a sure sign of the beautiful white-footed mouse.

abandoned birds' nests by capping them with a tightly woven grass roof. And while you might see the vole around during the day, these mice are almost entirely nocturnal. Their favorite foods are nuts and fruit pits, and the many stands of black cherry trees found on barrier beaches are sure to harbor many mice growing fat on the cherry pits.

Any stand of cherry or serviceberry trees will have its attendant white-footed mice, but observation is difficult because they are almost entirely nocturnal. Many of these mice live under the boardwalks of nature trails. Sometimes you will see tiny piles of refuse beside the boardwalks; these may be discarded cherry pits that had been gnawed by the mouse the previous night. A careful examination of the forest floor may reveal some partially eaten mushroom caps, the tiny teeth-marks evidence of a visit by the white-footed mouse.

Only after a snowfall does the abundance of white-footed mice become evident; their tiny, delicate tracks, looking like diminutive rabbit tracks, lace the thickets.

The **Meadow Jumping Mouse** *(Zapus hudsonius)* is an attractive little acrobat of the grassy fields and pocket meadows. The most noticeable feature of these mice is their tail, which is hairless and thin like a whip, and almost three times as long as their bodies. They have large and powerful hind legs with which, as their name implies, they can make prodigious leaps to escape their enemies. They have a bicolor pattern on their bodies; light yellowish brown at the top of their back, which changes midway down their sides to a much lighter beige. They have large ears and large black eyes, all which means this furtive little mouse leads an almost entirely nocturnal existence.

Another interesting departure from the other two mice we have discussed is that the jumping mouse goes into a deep hibernation at the ap-

Figure 45 The meadow jumping mouse is capable of six-foot leaps to escape its many enemies. Notice the powerful hind feet and the long, naked tail, which it uses as a rudder when it jumps.

proach of winter. Around the end of September, it goes on an eating binge and builds up a large reservoir of fat. Then it builds a cozy nest of woven grass about a foot beneath the sandy soil. Here it curls up in a tight ball and suspends its metabolism until its temperature is only a few degrees above freezing, its respiration is almost nonexistent and its heartbeat is reduced to a few beats per minute. In late April it digs itself out, almost immediately mates, and begins its frantic life of raising a family while trying to stay out of the way of the many predators that have this mouse on their menus.

All mice are subject to extreme population swings; one year the swales and pocket meadows of a barrier beach will be crawling with various species of mice, and another year they might be very rare. The meadow jumping mouse is no exception, and its population swings from abundant to rare about every three or four years. The best chance for observation is at night around the pocket meadows that sometimes develop in the more protected areas of the barrier beach. One moonless night I sat very still at the edge of one of these meadows and watched a weasel hunting in the grass. Suddenly several jumping mice exploded out of a grass clump, popping out like bed springs into the air. The weasel was momentarily confused by all the sudden activity but it finally sprang into action and pinned one unfortunate mouse, biting it on the back of the neck and killing it instantly. The weasel bounded off into the night with its prize.

I returned to that meadow often. Sitting quietly by the nest I soon had mice jumping and crawling all around me and was able to observe some fascinating behavior of these lovely little animals. They seem to relish grass seeds of all kinds; one even took to using my knee as a feeding station and didn't mind the glare of my flashlight as I watched its delicate front paws manipulate the grass seeds into its mouth.

Eastern Cottontail *(Sylvilagus floridanus)* is the most observed prey animal on many barrier beaches. An adult cottontail is about 16 inches long and weighs about 3 or 4 pounds. In summer their coat has a reddish hue, which changes to a more grizzled appearance in the winter months.

This rabbit has a mating cycle in March and September, although a doe (female) rabbit may have up to six litters in a year. Litter size runs from one to nine, with four or five young being the normal number. The doe makes a nest by scraping a depression in an open grassy area, not too far from cover. Once the young are born, she will nurse them and then cover them with grass and leave the area. The young have almost no odor, and a lucky fox or weasel must literally stumble over the nest to find them. Young rabbits are weaned at about twenty days, and then they're on their own, thrown into a world in which it seems every tooth and fang is against them.

Cottontail rabbits can be seen sunning themselves by the side of the road, or on any slope that favors a southern exposure, in the early

Figure 46 The ubiquitous cottontail rabbit is one of the most important prey animals on the barrier beach.

morning, or about an hour before sunset. They practice coprophagy, or reingestion of food. Green plant food is rapidly swallowed during feeding and the rabbit returns to protective cover where the food is defecated as soft, partially digested pellets. The rabbit can then re-eat the food at its leisure in a safe, hidden spot away from danger. Sometimes the rabbits' feeding areas are quite close to a road and they can be observed from your car, at close quarters, nibbling on new grass or spring clover.

Courtship is often a violent affair, with the bucks fighting viciously for the attention of the does. They often perform amazing acrobatic kicks and leaps during these fighting maneuvers, sometimes with deadly effect. That cute "Thumper" bunny is quite capable of inflicting serious injury or even disemboweling its adversary with karate-like kicks from its powerful hind feet.

Foxes, weasels, hawks and owls all hunt these rabbits. Some predators, especially hawks, are picky eaters, consuming only the choice internal organs and some haunch meat and leaving the rest after a kill. The abandoned rabbit carcass becomes a valuable source of protein for many animals, especially during the lean winter months.

The familiar **Muskrat** *(Ondatra zibethicus)* can be seen easily in many of the freshwater habitats that commonly occur on some barrier beaches. They are often numerous among the larger swales and ponds that rim the western edge of most barrier beaches. This close cousin of the beaver averages 18 to 20 inches in length (8 to 11 inches are tail) and weighs from 2 to 5 pounds. Its fur quality is outstanding, having a brown luster and a luxurious thickness to its pelt which is rivaled only by the mink. For this reason muskrats are trapped extensively in almost every area of America and Canada.

Many people see a muskrat swimming and mistake it for its close cousin, the beaver, but the beaver is much larger, with a broader head. The tail of the muskrat is its most notable characteristic; it is long and thin and laterally compressed (flat up and down), compared to the much larger flat tail of the beaver. Although it swims with its webbed back feet, the muskrat uses its tail as a scull in the water. When you see a muskrat swimming, you will almost always see its tail floating on the water's surface, but a beaver's tail is generally held under the water when it swims. Except in isolated wilderness areas, beavers are generally nocturnal animals, but muskrats are abroad during the daylight hours as well.

Muskrats build small lodges (known locally as "pushups") made of cattail leaves, grass, debris and some mud, all cleverly woven into watertight domes about two to three feet high. These are usually located in shallow freshwater areas and serve as dry nesting sites or food caches. If the right materials for lodge building are not available, the muskrat will dig a burrow into a mud bank. They also build extensive canals leading from their houses to prime feeding areas. This building activity helps keep the marsh open and the water flowing freely.

Muskrats are very prolific rodents, sometimes having as many as six litters a year, averaging one to nine young in a litter. Their population

Figure 47 The muskrat can often be observed at its feeding platform, which it usually makes out of flattened cattails or other grasses. This resourceful muskrat has taken advantage of a board that has floated into the marsh.

is cyclical; some years it seems every puddle has its attendant muskrat, while other years they will be noticeably absent. But their general abundance makes them important prey animals for the larger predators of the barrier beach. The fox takes many muskrats throughout the year, especially in the winter when the fox can safely walk across the ice to the lodges. I have seen some fox dens that were so littered with muskrat remains that it was evident the fox was feeding on muskrat exclusively. Hawks and owls sometimes snatch the young, although a full-grown muskrat is a tough and aggressive adversary, more than a match for all but the largest predators.

A fresh or brackish marsh is the place to see the muskrat. Muskrats often dive underwater and snip off cattail roots or other water plants and take them to a favorite feeding platform. These platforms are flattened areas of marsh vegetation that often contain plant cuttings and droppings. If you are lucky, you might see a muskrat cleaning its luxurious fur in the golden light of early morning.

The **Woodchuck** *(Marmota monax)* is very much like a fat squirrel that lives in burrows under the ground, rather than in trees, like true squirrels. Woodchucks are large, burrowing rodents, and can be seen easily feeding or sunning themselves in the larger grassy meadows of some barrier beaches. Unlike the squirrel, they eat no nuts, only the tender shoots of new plants, and grasses. They are master burrowers, digging out long and complex tunnels that have many emergency exits, and a chamber for hibernating and nesting. Their burrows serve as second-owner homes for other animals such as the fox, rabbit, weasel, and snake.

The woodchuck's weight swings from obese to downright scrawny. For six months of the year woodchucks gorge themselves to obesity, almost doubling their normal body weight. At the first sign of frost they retire into hibernation, subsisting only on their stored body fat. Six months later they emerge, weighing half as much as they did the previous summer.

The woodchuck is one of the most commonly seen wild animals on some barrier beaches. They are a familiar sight on the barrier

Figure 48 The woodchuck often sits upright to scan its feeding area for enemies.

beaches of New England, where drumlins anchor many of the beaches and the soil is composed of a mix of clay and sand. They prefer to construct their burrows in this type of soil rather than sand, which will collapse upon them. You will find their four to six-inch diameter holes, most with mounds of newly dug sand at the entrance, all over the interior dunes and upland areas of these barrier beaches.

No animal likes to be too far from protective cover, and woodchucks are no exception. During the early morning and late evening hours, they venture into open fields to eat succulent plants. They will often sit upright on their haunches to scan the area for enemies. This is an excellent time to observe their sometimes strange behavior. Large hawks occasionally take young woodchucks, and they seem especially fearful of any large, black object in the sky. I have seen them run in panic at the sight of an airplane!

Only the fox is powerful enough to feed regularly on the woodchuck, for an adult woodchuck is a fierce fighter. The young are sometimes taken by hawks, weasels and owls. Many are hit by cars in the spring when they wander long distances to find mates. Like rabbits and muskrats, woodchucks are susceptible to many debilitating diseases that cause some regional fluctuations in their population.

White-Tailed Deer (*Odocoileus virginianus*) inhabit the scrub and forested parts of many barrier beaches and islands. Deer are creatures of habit; they have their own home territories and well-traveled paths. You just have to locate these areas and be there at the right time to view these beautiful animals.

During the autumn the bucks' antler growth is complete, and they seem to relish rubbing their antlers against small trees and saplings to scrape off the velvet to hard bone. These antlers are the most rapid-growing bone tissue of any animal; it only takes four months to grow a complete set of antlers which may weigh several pounds.

Deer mate in November and the fawns are born in isolated thickets around the end of May. Many small, isolated swales are used for these birthing areas, for their covering of bayberry and poison ivy hides the fawn well.

The fox occasionally takes a fawn, but man and domestic dogs are the most dangerous enemy of deer on many barrier beaches. Before barrier beaches were settled, and the Indians were only summer visitors, wolves and cougars were the deer's chief enemies. Now, poaching is not uncommon on many barrier beaches, including some that are wildlife refuges. The situation is aggrevated by inconsiderate persons throwing apples and various "treats" (bananas, ice cream cones, gum, candy bars, etc.) into the fields to attract the deer. This practice lures the deer close to the road and needlessly habituates them to human contact. Their fear of humans gone, they make easy targets for poachers.

Sometimes a deer dies of starvation, disease, or just old age. Its carcass becomes an important

Figure 49 White-tailed deer are found on most barrier beaches that have extensive thicket and forest areas.

source of food for some predators, like the fox, and for scavengers, like the skunk, the crow and the herring gull.

Deer are easy to observe if you remember that they are creatures of habit and are most active during the early morning hours and at dusk. In spring and summer they like to congregate at dusk on upland fields. In autumn, look for small trees with long vertical gashes, evidence of antler rubbing or mock battles of the night before. During the heat of the day they retire to isolated thickets to chew their cud.

Wild Ponies are found on a few barrier beaches along the mid-and south-Atlantic coast; most notably on Assateague Island, Virginia, and Shackleford Island, North Carolina. There are other populations outside our study area on islands off of Goergia and Nova Scotia. No one is sure how the wild ponies arrived on Assateague Island. A traditional explanation states that a Spanish galleon, carrying horses to the colonies in South America, became shipwrecked in the late 1500s, and some of the horses escaped to begin their feral life on the Island. A less romantic, but more realistic, explanation, is that barrier islands were often used by early colonists to store their stock for the winter. Oxen, cattle, sheep, pigs and horses were all kept on barrier beaches over the winter, and then rounded-up when needed the next season. Some of the horses escaped the round-up and began to revert back to the wild.

Feral ponies that live on barrier beaches are usually smaller than normal-sized horses. Scientists speculate that their smaller size and compact build may derive from genetic adaptations to the windswept landscape and coarse vegetation of the barrier beach environment.

The wild ponies on Assateague Island are divided into two major ranges, the Maryland end of the Assateague Island National Seashore,

Figure 50 Wild ponies are found on a few islands of the Outer Banks.

and the Chincoteague herd that ranges on the Chincoteague National Wildlife Refuge. The Chincoteague herd is closely managed, and has been the focus of national attention due to the annual "penning" ceremony, which culls some of the foals from the main herd. These foals are auctioned off and the proceeds are applied to the upkeep of the main herd. The Maryland herd roams freely with no human intervention, and these ponies have established the stallion-dominated harems and other feral behavior associated with wild horses.

I have included wild ponies as prey animals in this section because they contribute to the overall ecology of barrier beaches in much the same way as would any other prey species. Wild horses are grazers; i.e., they grind up the grass they eat with large, flat teeth, and process the food in their highly specialized digestive systems. About 50% of their diet is saltwater cord grass, while the rest of their diet includes beach grass, poison ivy, rushes, phragmities, greenbriar, and many other kinds of grasses and shrubs. Deer prefer soft grasses, and become browsers during the winter months, eating much more bark and woody vegetation than wild ponies. Deer and wild ponies don't compete for the same foods on barrier beaches.

The everyday activities of wild ponies has an impact on the ecology of the thickets and marshes which comprise their territories. Being creatures of habit, they establish trails leading to and from watering holes and their feeding grounds. A thicket is often laced with pony trails, which become deep ruts after years of use. These trails are then used by other animals that live in the thickets, like the deer, raccoon, or fox.

Because the diet of wild ponies is poor in protein and other nutrients, they must eat about seventy pounds of grass each day. While most of their diet consists of salt marsh grasses, some herds seem to concentrate on beach grass. Eating and trampling the beach grass has produced severe erosion in small, isolated areas of Assateague Island. When the ponies defecate, they leave large piles of half-digested grasses, which return many nutrients back into the soil.

Wild ponies have developed beneficial relationships with other creatures that live on barrier beaches. When the ponies forage, they kick up insects that are eaten by the patient Cattle Egret *(Bubulcus ibis)*. This egret, although a native of Africa, has, in the last century, become widespread along the Atlantic coastline. Crows will also pick up insects stirred by the ponies' hooves. Black birds and grackles often patrol the backs of the ponies, picking off biting flies and ticks.

There are many more prey animals on barrier beaches, but those mentioned above are the most important and sustain the majority of predators. Some animals are both prey and predator; an example would be the skunk, which eats anything from birds' eggs to crickets, and is itself eaten by the great horned owl.

Predatory Animals of Barrier Beaches

Animal predators hunt and eat prey animals. By doing so, they gain the nutrients necessary to perpetuate themselves and their species. Ultimately, what they do as predators contributes to the continuance of the ecological structure in which they live. Predators probably have no concept of ecological balance; they're just worrying about their next meal. But by consuming prey animals, they not only control prey populations from becoming so large as to endanger the entire biological unit, but the waste products and leftovers from their kills help to enrich the soil and provide food for scavengers. Finally, their own death, whether by another, more powerful predator, or disease and old age, returns the nutrients of their own flesh back to the system from which it was first produced.

The Red Fox *(Vulpes vulpes)* is at the top of the food chain on barrier beaches. Although an adult usually weighs only about 8 to 12 pounds, the red fox is the most powerful and successful predator of its domain. It is the size of a small dog, with a long, pointed snout, large prominent ears and a long bushy tail. The red fox usually has fur which is a rich red color, although black and yellow color phases are not uncommon.

Foxes mate in January, during the coldest part of the winter, and both sexes will travel extensively to join up with a mate. They often spray their urine on the snow to attract a mate, and an alert walker can smell one of these scent-posts from many feet away in the crisp winter air. Their urine has a very strong odor, similar in smell to a mild skunk odor. At night, during the mating season, you may hear their terrier-like yips as they call to each other across the frozen dunes.

Figure 51 The fox prefers to stalk and pounce on its prey, much like a cat, instead of running it down, like its close cousin, the dog.

Foxes usually take over an old woodchuck hole, excavating a series of tunnels with several entrances. In March or early April four to ten young, or "kits," are born. The kits remain hidden inside the den with their mother until they are about four or five weeks old. During this time the male is an especially attentive father, constantly running back and forth from the den to the hunting areas, feeding not only himself but his hungry mate as well. In May the kits crawl to the outside and begin tentative explorations of their new world. One of the most endearing sights in nature is watching fox kits tumbling and playing outside their den entrance while their mother, ever alert, watches over them. By August the kits are almost fully grown, and they disperse to find their own hunting grounds.

The fox eats just about anything. As with most intelligent predators, the fox will exploit whatever is at hand, so cataloging a list of what is on its menu depends primarily on which season he is doing his hunting. In spring and summer the fox feeds on eggs, young birds, rabbits, mice, young woodchucks, pheasant, an occasional young fawn and insects. In fall and winter mice, rabbits and muskrats are the mainstays. Barrier beaches produce great amounts of edible berries every year, and berries are an important food item for the fox, which stuffs itself with blueberries, cherries, plums, raspberries and grapes when they are ripe.

The fox is a careful and intelligent animal, and one that does not like to be caught off its guard. To see a fox hunting is a real treat, but you will most likely know of its presence by its ubiquitous tracks, that tell of its nighttime travels. Unleashed dogs are not allowed in most National Wildlife Refuges or National Seashores, so any small dog-like track you find in the sand or snow will probably belong to the fox. Follow a fox track and it will lead you through many small sagas, which might include evidence of chases, digs, near misses and maybe the drama of a kill.

The fox hunts the ecological "edges" of the barrier beach; those transitional zones between the thicket and the forest, or between the forest and the salt marsh. These are the most productive areas for many of the small animals that the fox has on its menu. You may be able to spot a fox in the early morning hunting along the edge between the maritime forest and the salt marsh. Sometimes they become so intent upon the stalk and chase that you may be able to observe them without disturbing their hunting. Usually you will only see the signs of their presence; tracks of their hunting forays from the night before winding gracefully through the heather, or a ring of feathers and a bit of flesh, where the fox killed to feed its hungry kits.

The Short-Tailed Weasel *(Mustela erminea)* is, pound for pound, the most ferocious little terror in the forest. As a hunter of mice, it is without parallel and would put any cat to shame. Once its keen nose is locked onto the trail of the mouse, it is only a matter of time until the weasel dispatches its prey with a powerful bite on the back of the neck.

Weasels are long-bodied, short-legged little bundles of fury. They move by loping along with their backs arched, nose to the ground, sniffling for any scent of mice, their favorite prey.

The weasel owns two coats, a summer one that is chocolate brown on its back to cream on its stomach and under its chin. The winter coat is pure white except for an inch of black at the tip of its tail. The weasel in winter, with its white fur and its jet black eyes and tail tip, is a dazzling sight. It averages about 8 to 13 inches long, with a tail that is about half its body length. The males are somewhat larger than the females, but both sexes display the same aggressive abandon in their hunting techniques.

The weasel most often takes over an abandoned chipmunk burrow, or a shallow excavation beneath a log or a pile of rocks. The weasels' reproductive cycle is long; they mate in early summer, but the fertilized eggs lie dormant in the female for several months. She will wait to give birth to her four to nine tiny young until the following spring. The young's growth rate is incredibly fast; at five weeks old a young male is bigger than its mother!

Weasels have a diverse menu, depending upon the season. They will eat any small rodent, along with birds, eggs, reptiles, amphibians, insects and worms. But voles, mice and shrews are its main diet year-round. The weasel is also prey for some of the larger, more aggressive predators, such as the red fox, great horned owl or rough-legged hawk. Hunting this bundle of fury can have its drawbacks, however. Hawks have been found, still flying, with the teeth and skull of a weasel imbedded in their chest!

Short-tailed weasels are difficult to observe, not because they are so wary or shy, but because they inhabit the more isolated, densely wooded tracts of the thicket area. They seem to be abroad as often in the daytime as at night. They seem to like wet areas, for most of my sightings have been near swales, or the brushy border of the salt marsh. Catching sight of a weasel can lead to a rare adventure.

If found, they seem to take no notice of you, but continue their intense search for anything edible along the forest floor, oblivious to the fact that they might be sniffling along your shoe for a mouse scent! By staying a discreet distance away, I have been able to follow a hunting weasel through the forest for many hours. But beware! Never try to handle this attractive assassin, for a weasel can bite like a sewing machine and can, when pressed, emit an odor that rivals its close cousin, the skunk!

Other Interesting Predators

There are several important bird predators which can be observed easily on a barrier beach. The most important of these is the **Marsh Hawk** *(Circus cyaneous),* a bird of the marshes and low-lying fields. Marsh hawks hunt and nest on barrier beaches, and are visible throughout the day, coursing low over the dunes and fields. Their flight is very distinctive, for they are capable of greatly controlled slow glides just a few feet off the ground. They have a low wing load ratio; i.e., they can achieve great wing lift efficiency for their wing area and body weight. This allows them to stall-out in even the slightest breeze, and maneuver with great dexterity at very slow speeds.

The marsh hawks' hunting technique aids in their identification. They normally fly about twenty to thirty feet above the ground, with their wings held in a shallow "V". They have excellent hearing and eyesight and can spot the slightest movement in the grass. Marsh hawks can be seen easily at any time of the day coursing low over the swales and pocket meadows of the back dunes.

The **Great Horned Owl** *(Bubo virginianus)* is the largest, most powerful owl that nests on barrier beaches. At night it terrorizes the mice population, but it is also capable of taking rabbits and skunks. It rules the nighttime sky, but during the day it retires to roost in tall trees. Look for evidence of its kills throughout the dunes; it normally decapitates its victims. The large pellets of the great horned owl can often be found underneath its roosting tree.

The **Osprey** *(Pandion haliaetus)* is a fishing hawk well adapted for its role as a predator of fish. The soles of its feet have sharp, spiny bumps that help it grip its slippery prey. It hovers above the fish, and then plunges feet-first into the water, picking up the fish with its powerful talons.

Ospreys sometimes nest on platforms built on tall poles placed at the edge of the salt marsh by wildlife personnel. They are more commonly seen in the mid-Atlantic coastline, and I have seen their nests on the tops of dead loblolly pines and on the roofs of old duck blinds. Ospreys can be recognized during flight by their large size, hooked, hawk-like bill, and dark patches at the "wrist" under the wing.

Figure 52 The kestrel is an important predator of mice and small birds on many barrier beaches.

Figure 53 The osprey soars over the sound area behind the barrier beach, looking for fish to pluck from the water.

The **Sparrow Hawk** *(Falco tinnunculus)*, also known as the Kestrel, is a beautiful little falcon that hunts mice and small birds in open fields and grassy areas. It often sits on telephone poles or fence posts, using these places to make quick dives at prey. During its hunting flights, it will often hover in the air to observe some tell-tale movement in the grass. The sparrow hawk is an excellent mouser, but during the spring and summer it also takes many small song birds, snakes, frogs and toads, and even large insects like grasshoppers and beetles.

Swallows probably aren't thought of as predators, but they spend most of their waking hours catching flying insects. They eat enormous quantities of mosquitos and flies, along with any other flying insects they can cram into their mouths. Swallows are common barrier beaches, probably because their main diet is the large quantities of mosquitos and flies that inhabit the salt marsh. **Bank Swallows** *(Riparia riparia)* nest in tunnels dug into the face of eroding cliffs; **Barn Swallows** *(Hirundo rustica)* once nested on rocky ledges, but now nest almost exclusively in the eaves of buildings; **Tree Swallows** *(Iridoprocne bicolor)* nest in the holes of dead trees and in the swallow boxes

Figure 54 Tree swallows, one of several kinds of swallows that frequent barrier beches, are an important predator of mosquitos and flies.

erected by wildlife personnel. Swallows, along with purple martins, kingbirds, and different types of flycatchers, consume enormous quantities of insects every year to feed themselves and their hungry broods.

During migration season the swallows mass together into large groups, sometimes containing many thousands of birds. They descend upon the bayberry and wax myrtle, devouring the white, waxy fruits. Why the swallows, which are eaters of insects at other times of the year, eat these fruits just before migration, has remained a mystery until recently. At first it was thought that some substance in the fruits acted as a carthartic, ridding the swallows of harmful insect parasites before they began their migration flights. Analysis of various berries, including bayberry, has revealed that their fat content is considerably more than that of insects, and it appears that the swallows are gorging themselves on the berries to lay up fat reserves to fuel their long migratory flights.

Their maneuverability in flight is amazing. I have stood amidst a flock of swallows while they were feeding, snatching insects just inches from my face. Not only do they eat enormous quantities of flying insects, but their exuberant flight and happy, social chatter as they call to each other while flying endear them to many observers.

The **Burrowing Wolf Spider** (*Geolycosa* sp.) inhabits open, protected sand areas between dunes. Many wolf spiders range the forest floor, running down their prey with a quick rush and a pounce. But the burrowing wolf spider digs a long, narrow hole into the sand that can be up to eighteen inches deep. The spider lines the hole with fine silk so it won't collapse. The hole opens up at the end to form a bulb, in which the spider has its nest and a cavity to store its most recent victims.

It hunts by hanging at the entrance to its burrow, with just its eyes peeking over the edge. With its excellent eyesight and sensitive feet, the burrowing wolf spider can sense any potential prey, like a greenhead fly or a beetle, within a few feet from its burrow. Look for dime-sized holes in protected sand areas. You may be able to lure a spider out of its hole by sitting quietly and tickling a piece of grass over the sand. This movement imitates that of an injured insect, and may draw the spider out of the burrow. But look quickly, for these spiders are very fast and can disappear into their burrows in a flash!

In late summer, watch for a medium-sized, black-and yellow-striped wasp digging in open sandy areas in the dunes. This is the **Eastern Sand Wasp** (*Bembix americana*), one of the most fascinating creatures of the dunes. This wasp digs shallow tunnels into the sand that are used as storage chambers for its victims. It first digs a tunnel about 3 to 6 inches long into the sand, and then, after noting pertinent landmarks and making a "map" of the area in its memory, it flies off to find its victim, which may be several hundred yards away. Most often the victim is a fly of some sort, which the wasp paralyzes, and drags back to its chamber. It finds its way back to its chamber by referencing the "map" of the area in its primitive brain. The wasp deposits a single egg on its victim and closes the entrance to the tunnel by moistening the sand with its saliva and tapping it down with its head. It continues to provision the burrow for about a week after the wasp egg hatches. The larva feasts on its still-live victims at its leisure, finally metamorphosing into the adult wasp, which burrows out and flies free. Then the wasp immediately digs another chamber and starts the whole operation again.

The **Steel-Blue Cricket Hunter** *(Chlorion aerarium)* is another interesting burrowing wasp of the dunes. This wasp is considerably larger than the sand wasp, and is colored a beautiful dark blue that becomes irridescent in the sun. The cricket hunter wasp paralyzes field crickets, sand grasshoppers and other large insects, drags them into its burrow, deposits a single egg, and then backs out and closes the burrow.

This interesting and complex insect behavior can be seen during July and August on open, but protected, sand areas in the dunes.

Figure 55 This cricket hunter wasp has paralyzed a sand grasshopper. The grasshopper will be dragged down the wasp's nesting hole and into a special chamber. The grasshopper serves as fresh food for the wasp's developing larvae.

Scavengers

Almost all predators leave edible remains after a kill. These may be in the form of pieces of skin, internal organs, bones with flesh still attached, or even a whole carcass, if the animal has died accidentally, or of old age or disease. To obtain sustenance from this excess protein, certain animals have adapted their behavior to live almost entirely from these kill remains. Other animals are hunters but sometimes scavenge their meals.

Once a kill has been made, the stage is set for an intricate series of steps that results in the eventual reduction of the killed animal to its basic organic elements. Say, for example, that a fox has killed a rabbit and left some scraps after it has eaten. Soon these are discovered by the crows, which keep a keen eye out for anything they might scavenge. While the crows eat the remaining soft organic material—skin, viscera, brains, etc.—they leave behind the fur and bones. These, in turn, are eaten by mice, which chew on the bones for their calcium content, and by many kinds of insects, especially ants, which burrow into the bones and extract the marrow. Finally, chemical reduction due to weathering, and molds and bacteria, break down what's left over. Years later, a rabbit feeding in a pocket-meadow might be eating grass whose soil nurishment came from the reduced organic ingredients from the rabbit's ancester. And so goes the endless round of birth, death and renewal, with every living thing having an important role in the process.

If a kill is made in open sand, it soon becomes desiccated. Open sandy areas do not contain as many scavenging animals as grassy or shrubby areas, and the dry sand quickly draws out any moisture in the carcass. In summer it is common to find kills that have become mummified in the intense heat and dryness of the dunes.

The **Common Crow** (*Corvus brachyrhynchos*) is an active, highly intelligent bird, which is responsible for much of the scavenging activity

Figure 56 The crow is one of the most intelligent and resourceful animals of the barrier beach.

on barrier beaches. Several pairs usually nest in the furthest recess of the maritime forest, and groups of crows can be seen in the fall and winter patrolling their territories for the remains of kills. They are in visual contact with everything that goes on in a barrier beach, and are usually aware when a fox or hawk makes a kill.

The **Fish Crow** *(Corvus ossifragus)* is the southern crow, inhabiting the low coastal regions south of Massachusetts. Its habits are similar to the slightly larger common crow, but its range is almost exclusively limited to the seacoast. The fish crow replaces the common crow on the mid-Atlantic barrier beaches. The fish crow can be distinguished from the common crow by its slightly smaller size (although this is difficult to see in the field). The fish crow has a more "nasal"*kwok* than the sharp *caw!* of its northern relative.

The careful observer can often plot where other predators are by the activities of crows. If the fox is patrolling in the daytime, it is often followed by crows, and other small song birds, which announce its presence to the neighborhood. Crows are also notorious for mobbing owls that are incautious enough to be found in the daytime. Watch for a hawk on the ground eating a kill, and you will usually see several crows close by, waiting their turn for a meal.

The crow is an example of a scavenger that can also be an active predator. If it gets the chance, it will raid birds' nests, killing and eating the chicks or pecking open the eggs. It will also eat small snakes and insects.

The **Herring Gull** *(Larus argentatus)* is the ubiquitous gull seen perched atop pilings or pecking away at some tidbit on the beach. It keeps its scavenging confined mostly to the beach or the salt marsh, but it also occasionally feeds on kills found in the thickets and forests. Sometimes you will see them dropping clams or snails on a road, or other hard surface, to crack the hard shells. The herring gull has increased its range in recent years, probably due to the excess food available from dumps. It has pushed out more southern species common to barrier beaches, like the **Laughing Gull** *(Larus atricilla),* which is still common along the mid-Atlantic coast.

The **Striped Skunk** *(Mephitis mephitis)* needs no description. It is too well known by motorists who have to roll up their windows to avoid

Figure 57 The laughing gull, like its more northern neighbor the herring gull, is an important scavenger on barrier beaches.

the reek of a skunk killed on the road. Its population varies greatly, due to its susceptibility to rabies and other debilitating diseases. Having an excellent nose, it can smell out a kill at a considerable distance. The skunk's nose is so sensitive it can even smell out kills buried under the sand by the fox.

It will eat just about anything, from scavenging a deer carcass to raiding the eggs of a bird's nest. In the summer it eats enormous quantities of crickets and ground beetles. The coldest days of winter force it to seek shelter in an abandoned woodchuck hole, where it will go into a stupor—not true hibernation—until the weather is milder.

Skunks are basically nocturnal creatures, but in the summer they start their forays in the early evening and it is common to see several shuffling through the grass in the upland areas. They use the random-search technique for finding something to eat—they just snuffle along until their nose leads them to some food.

Probably the most inquisitive animal on the barrier beach is the **Raccoon** *(Procyon lotor)*. Its curiosity is directly connected to its stomach, for the raccoon is constantly on the lookout for an easy meal. Barrier beaches offer the intelligent and resourceful raccoon a banquet of foods to choose from, with several kinds of berries, shellfish, grapes, small mammals, young birds, eggs, insects, snakes and carrion—just a few items on its ever-expanding menu.

Raccoons frequent ecological "edges," and they are most common along the border between the maritime forest and the salt marsh. Adult raccoons defend their territories fiercely against intrusion by other raccoons, and I have been awakened in my tent on many nights by their raucous squabbling. One of their favorite passtimes is digging for shellfish along the marsh creeks at low tide. They often leave piles of clam and oyster shells on the creek banks as evidence of their nighttime feasts.

Figure 58 The wily raccoon is an intelligent and curious creature, and it takes full advantage of the food resources found on a barrier beach.

Coda

So much of our lives are lived within the boundaries of the environment that we've created that we think it is exceptional when we visit places that are "real" wilderness—we have the sinking feeling that wilderness areas just don't care if we're present or not; they're going to continue their ancient ways despite us. I can still get that feeling walking the winter beach on Cape Cod, or poling a canoe through the marsh creeks on Assateague Island.

Barrier beaches have a tragic history of abuse, from allowing livestock to chew the vegetation down to the bare sand, to using them as the basis of real estate scams for the gullible and unwary. With few exceptions, barrier beaches are examples of abused land healing itself. Early accounts suggest that the flora and fauna found on barrier beaches was much richer and more diversified than today. After colonization, many barrier beaches rapidly declined. The early settlers quickly removed any usable timber, and burned large tracts to open up thicket areas and promote the growth of forage grasses. Farmers penned their half-feral stock on barrier beaches, primarily to escape the pervasive colonial taxes levied against fencing, and the pigs, goats, cows, oxen, and horses proceeded to trample and eat the place down to bare sand. Plum Island, off the coast of Massachusetts, is only one of many barrier beaches abused in this manner. Thoreau, after a tramp down the length of the Island, remarked that he did not see any tree or shrub taller than three feet growing anywhere.

With the establishment of the extensive National Seashores and the numerous Federal Wildlife Refuges along the coast, many of the most beautiful of our barrier beaches have been saved from further destruction. Some sections of these preserved barrier islands contain pockets of the original maritime forests, such as Buxton Woods and Nag's Head Woods on Cape Hatteras, North Carolina, or the Sunken Forest on Fire Island, New York.

Many important pieces of legislation were passed in the 1970s that protected barrier beaches. The Coastal Zone Management Act of 1972 created an umbrella agency that dispenses help in the form of funds, programs and guidance to state agencies involved in protecting our coastal areas. Other Federal programs, like the Endangered Species Act of 1973, the Federal Water Pollution Control Act of 1972, the Water Resources Development Act of 1974, the Clean Air Act of 1970, the Environmental Pesticide Control Act of 1972, the Marine Protection, Research, and Sanctuaries Act of 1972, and the Clean Water Act of 1977, have all added necessary programming and funding to insure the protection of our barrier beaches. Many states have added their own legislation which limits development on barrier beaches.

But we can't expect state and federal authorities to accept the sole responsibility for maintaining our barrier beaches. Every person who lives upon or merely visits a barrier beach must accept a moral responsibility regarding use of these fragile areas. The future will only bring increasing population pressures to develop our limited coastal areas.

This responsibility might be better understood if we realize how unique and fragile barrier beaches really are. Barrier beaches are unique because their various ecosystems exist so close together. Pocket freshwater marshes exist within a few-score yards of the ocean. The parched, desert-like dunes loom over the eternally wetted saltmarsh. These seemingly opposite ecological areas can be easily experienced in an hour's walk across almost any barrier beach.

We tend to see barrier beaches as static places and build what we think are permanent dwellings upon the sand. In reality all barrier beaches are temporary, and are constantly shifting and moving according to the laws of surf, tide and wind. One storm can drastically change a barrier beach forever, and yet we seem vaguely surprised when a northeaster or hurricane severely damages these fragile ocean margins.

Even the words we use to describe natural processes betray our inability to deal with the forces of the shoreline on their own terms. "Erosion" is a word we use for the sea wearing away sections of the beach, encroaching upon our control and possession of the coast. Actually, "erosion" doesn't exist in nature, it is simply the shoreline adjusting to a rising sea level. We call it erosion when a storm surge topples our houses or undermines our seawalls. Erecting walls will not stop the rising sea level. We must come to terms with the fact that there is *nothing we can do* to stop the rising sea level. We should listen to coastal scientists instead of developers concerning the future of our coastal resources. Barrier beaches are going to move out from under our homes and our towns no matter how many sea walls, groins, and jetties we build to try and stop it. These are all, at best, temporary measures.

Although a barrier beach may not fit our preconceived ideas about what is wilderness, it is bordered by the immutable ocean, the largest unexplored wilderness on earth. Without technological aid, we could no more live in the ocean than we could in outer space. The ocean is the progenitor of the barrier beach; its waves cull the sand into form. Its storms shape the dunes like a potter rubbing up the clay. The barrier beach flexes and shifts, becoming the expression of the forces of ocean and wind upon the land, and in their art, we discover the exotic and the incomprehensible.

Suggested Bibliography

Amos, W.H. 1985. *Assateague Island,* National Park Handbook #106. Washington, D.C.: Superintendent of Documents, U.S. Government Printing Office.

Amos, W.H.; Amos, S.H. 1985. *Atlantic & Gulf Coasts,* Audubon Society Nature Guides. New York: Alfred A. Knopf.

Arnold, A.F., 1901. *The Sea-Beach at Ebb Tide.* 1968. New York: Dover Publications, Inc.

Bascom, W. 1964. *Waves and Beaches,* Garden City, N.Y.: Doubleday and Co. Inc.

Behler, J.L.; King, F.W. *The Audubon Society Field Guide to North American Reptiles and Amphibians,* New York: Alfred A. Knopf.

Berrill, M.; Berrill, D. 1981. *The North Atlantic Coast,* A Sierra Club Naturalist's Guide. San Francisco, Sierra Club Books.

Berrill, N.J.; Berrill, J. 1957. *1001 Questions Answered About the Seashore,* New York: Dover Publications.

Bird, E.C.F. 1969. *Coasts,* Cambridge, Mass.: MIT Press.

Borror, D.J.; White, B. 1970. *A Field Guide to the Insects of America North of Mexico,* Peterson Field Guide Series. Boston, Mass.: Houghton Mifflin Co.

Brown, L. 1979. *Grasses, An Identification Guide,* Boston: Houghton Mifflin Co.

Carlson, B.S.; Godfrey, P.J. *An Ecological Evaluation of Human Impact on the Crane's Beach Reservation, Ipswich, Mass.* Amherst, Mass.: Univ. of Carson, R. 1955. *The Edge of the Sea,* Boston, Mass.: Houghton Mifflin Co.

Chamberlain, B.B. 1964. *These Fragile Outposts,* Yarmouth Port, MA.: Parnassus Imprints.

Clark, J. 1977. *Coastal Ecosystems Management,* New York: John Wiley & Sons.

Coates, D. (ed.). *Coastal Geomorphology,* Binghampton, N.Y.: Publications in Geomorphology, State University of New York, 1972.

Conant, R. 1975. *Field Guide to Reptiles and Amphibians of Eastern and Central North America,* Peterson Field Guide Series, Boston, Mass.: Houghton, Mifflin Co.

Cronon, W. 1983. *Changes in the Land.* New York: Farrar, Straus and Giroux.

Crosland, Patrick D. *The Outer Banks,* Arlington, Va.; Interpretive Publications, 1981.

Currier, J.J. 1896. *Ould Newbury,* Boston, Mass.: Damrell and Upham; reprinted, Newburyport, MA.: Park River Researchers, pp. 212-220.

Ducsik, D.W. 1974. *Shoreline for the Public,* Cambridge, Mass.: The MIT Press.

Emerton, J.H. 1961. *The Common Spiders of the United States,* New York: Dover Publications, Inc.

Epply, A.O. 1983. *The Amphibians of New England,* Camden, Maine: Down East Books.

Evans, H.E. 1963. *Wasp Farm,* Garden City, N.Y.: Doubleday and Co. Inc.

Fox, W.T. 1983. *At the Sea's Edge,* Englewood Cliffs, N.J.: Prentice-Hall, Inc.

Gates, D.A. 1975. *Seasons of the Salt Marsh,* Old Greenwich, Conn.: The Chatham Press.

Gosner, K.L. 1978. *A Field Guide to the Atlantic Seashore,* The Peterson Field Guide Series. Boston, Mass.: Houghton Mifflin Co.

Hamilton, W.J. and Whitaker, J.O., Jr. 1979. *Mammals of the Eastern United States,* Ithaca and London: Cornell University Press.

Harris, E.J. 1977. *Documents, Legends, and Archaeology: Unraveling the Mysteries of Newburyport's Past,* Palisades, CA.: Historical Survey Assoc.

Hay, J.; Farb, P. 1966. *The Atlantic Shore,* Orleans, Mass., Parnassus Imprints.

Hoyt, J. 1967. *Barrier Island Formation,* Geol. Soc. Amer. Bull., V. 78, p. 1125-1136.

Hruby, T.; Montgomery, W.G. *The Mosquito, the Salt Marsh, and You,* Gloucester, MA.: Resources for Cape Ann, Mass. Audubon Society.

Jackson, T.C., Oceanic Society, and Reische, D. ed. 1981. *Coast Alert,* San Francisco, CA: Friends of the Earth.

John, M.E. 1983. *Fire Island, 1650's-1980's,* Mountainside, N.J.: Shoreland Press.

Kaufman, Wallace, and Pilkey, Orrin. *The Beaches Are Moving.* Garden City, N.Y.: Anchor Press/ Doubleday, 1979.

Keipe, R.R. 1985. *The Assateague Ponies,* Centreville, Maryland: Tidwater Publishers.

Ketchen, B.H. 1972. *The Water's Edge,* Cambridge, Mass.: The MIT Press.

Kopper, P. 1979. *The Wild Edge, Life and Lore of the Great Atlantic Beches,* New York: Penquin Books.

Lazell, J.D. 1976. *This Broken Archipelago,* New York: The New York Times Book Co.

Leatherman, S.P. 1979. *Barrier Island Handbook,* College Park, Maryland: University of Maryland.

Leonard, J.W. 1972. *Atlantic Beaches,* New York: Time-Life Books Inc.

Lindberg, A.M. 1975. *Gift From the Sea,* New York: Random House.

Long, S.P.; Mason, C.F. 1983. *Saltmarsh Ecology,* London: Blackie. Distributed in U.S. New York: Methuen, Inc.

Mabbutt, J.A. 1977. *Desert Landforms,* Cambridge, Mass.: The MIT Press.

McDonnell, M.J. *The Flora of Plum Island, Essex County, Massachusetts,* Durham, New Hampshire: Agricultural Experiment Station, University of New Hampshire.

Murryman, J.H. 1981. *The United States Life-Saving Service-1880,* Golden, Colorado: Outbooks.

Milne, L.; Milne, M. 1980. *The Audubon Society Field Guide to North American Insects and Spiders,* New York: Alfred A. Knopf.

Morris, P.A. 1975. *A Field Guide to Shells of the Atlantic and Gulf Coasts and the West Indies,* The

Peterson Field Guide Series. Boston, Mass.: Houghton Mifflin Co.

Mulliken, S.E. *Plum Island,* Essex Institute Historical Collections vol. 88, no. 2 (April 1951). pp. 99-113.

Nichols, R.L. *Shoreline Changes on Plum Island, Mass.,* Journal of Science, vol. 240 (May 1942): pp. 349-355.

Ogburn, C. 1966. *The Winter Beach,* New York: William Morrow and Co., Inc.

Perry, B. 1985. *The Middle Atlantic Coast,* Sierra Club Naturalist's Guide. San Francisco: Sierra Club Books.

Pierce, J. 1970. "Tidal Inlets and Washover Fans", *Journal of Geology,* V. 78, p. 230-234.

Pilkey, O.H. Jr.,; Neal, W.J.; Pilkey, O.H. Sr.; Riggs, S.R. 1980. *From Currituck to Calabash,* Research Triangle Prak, N.W.: North Carolina Science and Technology Research Center.

Potter, C.E. 1856. *History of Manchester,* Manchester: C.E. Potter, Publisher, pp. 22-31.

Rau, P.; Rau, N. 1918. *Wasp Studies Afield.* 1970. New York: Dover Publications, Inc.

Rehder, H.A. 1981. *Audubon Society Field Guide to North American Seashells,* New York: Alfred A. Knopf.

Robbins, S.F.; Yentsch, C. 1973. *The Sea is All Around Us,* Salem, Mass.: Peabody Museum of Science.

Robbins, C.R.; Ray, G.C. 1986. *A Field Guide to Atlantic Coast Fishes of North America,* The Peterson Field Guide Series. Boston, Mass.: Houghton Mifflin Co.

Schwartz, M. 1971. *The Multiple Causality of Barrier Islands,* Journal of Geology, V. 79, p. 91-94.

Silberhorn, G.M. 1982. *Common Plants of the Mid-Atlantic Coast, A Field Guide,* Baltimore and London: John Hopkins University Press.

Simon, A.W. 1978. *The Thin Edge, Coast and Man in Crisis,* New York: Harper and Row Publishers, Inc.

Spencer, E.W. 1983. *Physical Geology*, Reading, Mass. Addison-Wesley Publishing Co.

Steers, J.A. 1971. *Applied Coastal Geomorphology*, Cambridge, Mass.: The MIT Press.

Swenson, A.A. 1981. *Secrets of a Seashore*, Portland, Me.; Guy Gannett Publishing Co.

Thoreau, H.D. 1864. *Cape Cod,* 1984. ed. Orleans, Mass.: Parnassus Imprints, Inc.

Truitt, R.V. 1971. *Assateague . . . the Place Across,* Center for Environmental and Estuarine Studies. University of Maryland.

U.S. Dept. of Agriculture, *Building, Planning, and Maintaining Coastal Sand Dunes,* Conservation on Information #32. Soil Conservation Service.

U.S. Fish and Wildlife Service, 1982. *Parker River National Wildlife Refuge Master Plan,* Environmental Impact Statement, Draft. Newton Corner, Mass.: Department of the Interior.

White, L.B. Jr. 1960. *Life int he Shifting Dunes,* Boston, Mass.: Museum of Science.

Wylie, F.E. 1979. *Tides and the Pull of the Moon,* Brattleboro, VT: Stephen Greene Press.

Index

Barrier beaches, formation of, 27, 28
Barrier beach migration, 25, 40-44, *38, 39*
Bayberry, 62, 63, *63*
Beach drift, 28, *29*, 30
Beach grass, 50-55, *50, 52, 53, 54*
Beach heather, 57, 58, *58*
Beach pea, 56, *56*, 57
Beach plum, 63, 64, *64*
Berms, 25
Blood worms, 90, 91
Blue mussel, 88
Burrowing wolf spider, 123

Cape Hatteras National Seashore, 3
Cheniers, *27*
Common crow, 125, 126, *126*

Dusy miller, 61, *61*, 62
Dynamic equilibrium, 22-27

Earth star fungus, 72, 73
Eastern cottontail, 105, 106, *106*
Eastern sand wasp, 123

Fire Island, 3, 4, 5, 11
Fish crow, 126, 127
Fowler's Toad, 75

Glaciation, 17
        of coasts, 16-20
Godfrey, Paul, 41
Great horned owl, 120
Green crab, 91
Greenhead fly, 94, 97, 98

Herring gull, 127
Hydrobia minuta, 90

Indians, 9-14

Laughing gull, 127, *127*
Lichen, 72
Life saving service, 5-7
Loblolly pine, *78, 79*
Longshore currents, 28, 29, *29*

Maritime forest, 77-81, *78, 79, 80*
Marsh hawk, 119

Meadow jumping mouse, 103-105, *104*
Meadow vole, 100, *101*, 102
Mummichog, 93
Muskrat, 107, 108, *108*

Nags Heads Woods, *79*, 80, *80*, 81

Osprey, 120, *121*
Overwash, *26*, 36, *38*, *39*, 43, 44

Pirates, 4, 5
Pitch pine, 78, 79
Plum Island, 2, 5, 9, 19, 20, 28, 74
Poison ivy, 58, 59, *59*
Ponies, 112-114, *113*
Prickly pear cactus, 73, *74*

Raccoon, 128, *129*
Red fox, 115-117, *116*
Ribbed mussel, 88, *89*

Saltation, 33
Salt marsh, 94-99, *84*, *99*
Salt marsh fish,
        mummichog, 93,
        stickleback, 93
Salt marsh food chain, 87-92
Salt marsh mosquito, 94-97
Salt marsh pools, 93
Salt marsh snail, 98
Salt meadow grass, 86
Saltspray, 65, *65*
Saltwater cord grass, 86
Saltworks, 8
Sand, composition of, 33, 34
Seaside goldenrod, 60, *60*
Shipwrecks, 5
Shrub/thicket community, 71-76, *71*
Smith, Captain John, 9, 10
Sparrow hawk, *120*, 121
Steel-blue cricket hunter wasp, 124, *124*
Storms, 35, 36-40
Striped skunk, 127, 128
Surface micro-climate, 47
Swales, 66-70, *67*, *69*
Swallows, 121-123, *122*

Tiger beetle, 75

Wampum, 11, 12

Wave refraction, *29*
Weasel, 117-119
Woodchuck, 109, *109,* 110
Whaling, 12
Whelk, 90
White-footed mouse, 102, *102,* 103
White-tailed deer, 75, 110-112, *111*
Wreckers, 3, 4

Picture Credits

Michael L. Hoel: 1, 4, 10, 11, 13, 16, 17, 18, 26, 28, 29, 30, 31, 32, 33, 34, 37, 38, 40, 41, 43, 44, 48, 50, 53, 55, 57, 58.

Kathleen MacDonald: 3, 15, 19, 20, 21, 22, 23, 24, 25, 39.

John Gavin: 14, 45, 46, 47, 49, 51, 52, 54, 56.

Michael Prendergast: 5, 6, 35, 36, 42.

Edith Heyck: 7, 8, 9, 12.

Bill Lane: cover photograph of Plum Island, Massachusetts.

Ralph Scott: back cover illustration of Snowy Owl.

Images of the Past: 2.